THE COMPLETE STORY

OTHER TITLES IN THE CROWOOD AUTOCLASSICS SERIES

MATTHEW VALE

ALVIS

THE COMPLETE STORY

THE CROWOOD PRESS

First published in 2019 by
The Crowood Press Ltd
Ramsbury, Marlborough
Wiltshire SN8 2HR

www.crowood.com

British Library Cataloguing-in-Publication Data
A catalogue record for this book is available from the British Library.

ISBN 978 1 78500 587 9

Designed and typeset by Guy Croton Publishing Services,
West Malling, Kent

Printed and bound in India by Parksons Graphics

CONTENTS

INTRODUCTION AND ACKNOWLEDGEMENTS

Even before Alvis cars ceased production in 1967, they had a mystique about them as a British marque which was always a cut above the mainstream. *Autocar* magazine summed this up in 1952 with the words: 'The Alvis has never been an ordinary car for the masses, but a mount for the sporting and discerning driver interested in a quality product, and in a car that still looks like a car and is ruggedly built.'

So the Alvis car had made a fine reputation for the company and this reputation was reinforced by Alvis's military vehicles and aero engines – both areas in which Alvis excelled and reinforced its reputation for engineering integrity. Alvis has left behind a lasting legacy of its cars, which are ably supported by Red Triangle and the owners clubs and registries across the globe, its classic radial aero engines and a range of innovative military vehicles, many of which are still in service around the world today.

This book looks at the Alvis company and describes its cars, military vehicles and aero engines up to time when Alvis finally relinquished its independence with the takeover by Rover and its eventual assimilation into British Leyland.

This book would not have been possible without the input from a large number of people and institutions and I would like to thank the following: the Alvis Owner Club and the owners of cars featured in this book for access to their cars and stories – Jonathan Huggett, Mike and Tricia Harcourt, Adam and Clare Gilchrist, Debby Gold, Edmund Waterhouse and Martin Slatford.

A special mention is given to Tony Cox for his information on the FWD cars and for taking the time to review my writing on the FWD cars. Also to Richard Joyce, Managing Director of Red Triangle, who put up with me for several hours and gave me a fascinating and informative tour of Red Triangle's premises.

I would also like to thank the Tank Museum, Bovingdon, for access to archive photos of some of the early Alvis military vehicles; the Aldershot Military Museum for access to its collection of Alvis armoured vehicles; and the British Motor Museum at Gaydon for access to the Alvis GTS, Rover P6BS and Graber Super Alvis pictured.

Finally, thanks are due to my wife Julia and daughter Elizabeth for putting up with me writing yet another book.

Matthew Vale
2019

CHAPTER ONE

THE ALVIS COMPANY
FROM 1919 TO 1939

INTRODUCTION

Alvis was one of those typically British car companies that grew up after World War I to provide the burgeoning middle classes with an affordable means of transport that was a cut above the norm. Based in the UK in the Midlands city of Coventry, the company offered cars with excellent engineering, impeccable style and a reassuringly high price tag. During the interwar years, Alvis made relatively small numbers of cars, which were clothed by the best coachbuilders of the day. Before World War II, the company had expanded into the production of aero engines and light armoured vehicles, and wartime production included bomb lifts, licence production and overhaul of Rolls-Royce Merlin and Kestrel aero engines, plus the manufacture of assorted aircraft parts and ground equipment.

After World War II, the company continued to develop its own aero engines, resulting in the successful Leonides family of radials, as well as producing a new range of cars

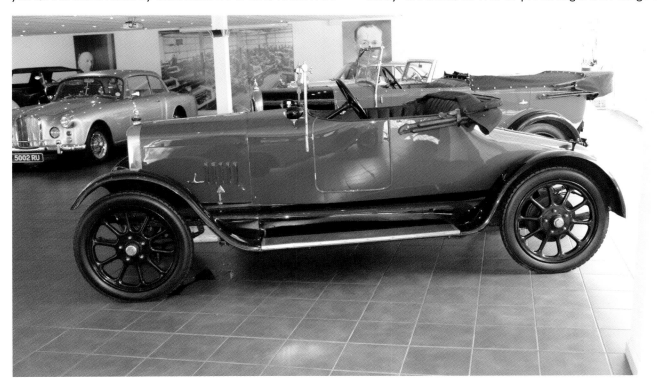

The first Alvis cars were the 10/30 side-valve models. This 1922 works model was pictured at Red Triangle's showroom in Warwickshire.

ALVIS COMPANY TIMELINE – 1919 TO 1945

Date	Event
Mar 1919	T.G. John purchases Holley Brothers Ltd, renaming the company T.G. John & Co. Ltd. Production of bodies for Zenith Carburettors, Hillman 4hp and 7hp stationary engines and Stafford Mobile Pup scooters started. Based in Hertford Street, Coventry
1919	John agrees to license G.P.H. de Freville's 4-cylinder 1.5-litre side-valve engine design and the Alvis name
Mar 1920	First 10/30 car produced using the de Freville engine
Mid-1920	Machine shop on Holyhead Road, Coventry, acquired
Late 1920	New machine tools and site on Holyhead Road, Coventry, acquired, as well as foundry on Lincoln Street, Coventry
Apr 1921	Works moved from Hertford Street to Holyhead Road Site
Dec 1921	T.G. John Ltd renamed the Alvis Car and Engineering Company Ltd
1921	11/40 produced as a cheaper version of the 10/30
1922	Production of the Buckingham Cycle Car commenced
1922	12/40 model introduced, replacing the 11/40
1922	Captain George Thomas Smith-Clark joins Alvis as Chief Engineer, Chief Designer and Works Manager
Late 1922	Overhead-valve version of the de Freville engine development started
Jun 1923	10/30 introduced with 1460cc ohv engine
Late 1923	12/50 supersedes 10/30 with ohv engine
1924	Front-wheel brakes offered as an option
Jun 1924	Cross and Ellis petitioned Alvis for monies owed, leading to liquidation of the company
Feb 1925	Receiver agrees rescue plan for Alvis, with creditors paid in cash or debentures
1925	Development of front-wheel drive technology commenced
1926	Straight-8 engine for FWD racers developed
1927	The 6-cylinder 14.75 based on the 12/50 chassis introduced

Date	Event
1928	First FWD road cars produced
1928	New service shop, machine shop and foundry building completed at Holyhead Road
1929	Silver Eagle 6-cylinder car replaced 14/75. Extension to factory built to address increased production needed to meet demand for Silver Eagle
1932	Speed 20 6-cylinder car introduced
Mid-1932	The 4-cylinder Firefly introduced to replace the 12/50
May 1933	Crested Eagle with fully independent front suspension introduced
Sep 1933	New all-synchromesh gearbox introduced
1934	Development of 8-cylinder road engines ended
Aug 1935	Negotiation with Gnome-Rhône for licences to manufacture aero engines successfully completed
1935	Firebird introduced to replace Firefly
1936	6-cylinder 3½-litre Speed 25 introduced, replacing the Speed 20
Jun 1936	Company name changed to Alvis Ltd
Jul 1936	New factory opened next to existing plant on Holyhead Road aimed primarily at aero- engine production
Jul 1936	Alvis-Straussler Mechanisation Ltd formed to produce Straussler designs of armoured cars and tanks
1936	New 4.3-litre 6-cylinder engine introduced along with Alvis 4.3 and Silver Crest
Sep 1937	12/70 introduced with new 4-cylinder engine
1938	Air Ministry informs Alvis that there would be no contracts for Gnome-Rhône based engines. Licence with Gnome-Rhône terminated. Development of Leonides started
Sep 1939	All Alvis production turned over to war work
Nov 1940	Original Alvis factory bombed and largely destroyed
Apr 1941	Aero-engine factory hit by Luftwaffe with some damage and casualties
1945	War ends and peacetime production begins.

The last Alvis car made was this TF21 Three Litre Series IV saloon, owned by Adam Gilchrist.

and developing a new family of six-wheeled military vehicles. Alvis was bought by Rover in 1965, but car production had ended by 1967, when Mulliner Park Ward could no longer supply TF21 bodies at an economic price.

Production of the six-wheeled military vehicles continued and the design of a new range of light tracked Armoured Fighting Vehicles (AFVs) commenced in 1967 with the Combat Vehicle Reconnaissance Tracked (CVRT) project, which would give birth to the Scorpion range of AFVs for the British Army.

EARLY DAYS AND THE 'ROARING TWENTIES'

The man responsible for setting up Alvis and running the company through to 1945 was Thomas George John, MINA, MICA, FRAeS, MIAE and ARCS. Born in 1880 in Pembroke Dock in south-west Wales, where John's father was employed in the Pembroke Royal Dockyard, John was apprenticed into the dockyard. He had become a qualified Naval Architect (MINA – Member of the Institute of Naval Architects) by 1904. He was promoted to the rank of Assistant Constructer at H.M. Dockyard Devonport, but left the Dockyards to join shipbuilders Vickers in 1907, where he was made Manager of the Shipbuilding Department in 1911.

The first Alvis engine was designed by de Freville and was a side-valve straight-4. Note the 'T.G. John' script cast into the alloy water jacket on the top of the cylinder head. Later cars would have 'Alvis' cast in.

DEBBY GOLD'S 1963 TE21

One of the recurring aspects I came across while writing this book was the deep impression that Alvis ownership has made on generations of people. Time and time again while chatting to owners, I discovered a deeply held affection for the cars and in many cases cross-generational ownership, with cars passing down the family line.

One classic example is Debby Gold's 1963 TE21 convertible, which was fitted with the Alvis straight-6 engine and a ZF five-speed manual gearbox. It was painted a striking metallic light beige with beige trim. Debby's father, Peter Gold, bought the car in 1969 from Hurst Park Automobiles in East Molesey, Surrey. Debby recalls how her dad, an engineer and successful businessman, always had a nice car, and the Alvis replaced a little black Series 1 Jaguar E-Type drophead with a red interior. Finding that the E-Type was encouraging his 'enthusiastic' driving style, he decided he needed more of a Grand Tourer, especially as his family was growing. Debby still remembers a trip down to Cornwall in the E-Type with her mum, herself and the family dog all crammed into the Jaguar. When Peter saw the Alvis he was hooked and paid around £1,200 for it – a fair sum in the late 1960s, when a new Mini cost under

£1,000 and a new E-Type roadster was just over £2,000.

Debby's dad loved the car and ran it as his high days and holidays car for many years, as he had two Humber Super Snipes as daily drivers, but eventually it was taken off the road in 1976 as the brakes needed repair. Distracted by another project and needing garage space, Peter relocated the car to Debby's garage in Hampshire. His health deteriorated and unfortunately renovating the Alvis became a bridge too far. He passed away in 1996.

Over the years, the car gently deteriorated, much to Debby's frustration, but every time she saw it, even looking sad and half covered with junk, it still reminded her of her dad. She vowed to get the car back on the road and in 2015 finally had the resources to commission a full restoration. The car had suffered while sitting in the garage. One side of the bodywork was significantly worse than the other due to damp getting through the wall of the garage. Debby made the decision to go for a concours restoration rather than just getting the car roadworthy, as the increased cost of a 100-point restoration would hopefully be offset by the value of an immaculate car. The car was exhumed from the garage where it had rested

Debby Gold's TE21 Three Litre convertible just after her father Peter Gold had bought it in 1969.

Debby Gold's TE21 was metallic beige with a beige interior. The car was used for high days and holidays rather than as a daily driver and plays a special part of Debby's family memories.

The TE21 had a distinctive nose with its pair of stacked headlights flanking the traditional Alvis grille. This is Debby Gold's car in the 1960s.

(continued overleaf)

continued from previous page

ABOVE: **Debby Gold's TE21 engine is the original 6-cylinder unit and was completely rebuilt as part of a comprehensive restoration.**

The restoration of **Debby Gold's TE21** required extensive bodywork repairs, as well as a full mechanical overhaul. Still in primer, the nose of the car now shows no evidence of the rust and rot that had taken hold during its long period in storage.

With the restoration nearly finished and the car back in her rebuilt garage, Debby is just sorting out the last few bits and bobs.

for nearly forty years and taken to a local classic Jaguar specialist's workshop for the transformation.

The car has since been treated to a full and exhaustive nut and bolt restoration, which covered everything. The good news was that the chassis was in relatively good condition and only needed localized repairs and a good clean-up and repaint. The suspension and running gear only needed rebushing, cleaning up and painting, along with the replacement of all rubber components. The engine had seized and required a complete rebuild, which, while costing less than doing a Jaguar XK unit, was still not cheap, but it was the bodyshell which really cost. The years sitting in the damp garage meant that much of the body had to be recreated, which cost both time and money and needed a great deal of skill to get it right. While some repair panels were available, much had to be recreated from scratch, but the end result was worth it.

Debby refurbished the leather seats herself, which had survived remarkably well and add a nice touch of original patina to the interior and the hood. The hood's ash frame in particular caused a lot of problems – there

is no 'one type fits all' solution here, as each hood frame was individually tailored to the car, so replacing the rotted wood elements of the frame and getting a new hood made were another costly exercise in time, effort and craftsmanship. With a new set of chrome wire wheels to offset the all new metallic beige paintwork, the TE21 looks a million dollars, and Debby is really happy with the result, despite some rocky moments towards the end of the restoration when the costs were escalating and progress seemed slow.

The cost of the restoration ended up being in six figures in pounds sterling, but Debby feels it was worth it – and she knows there was not a lot of choice other than to see it through once started. She has an immaculate car that evokes many great childhood memories, especially those connected with her dad and mum, and Debby is planning to take the car to as many Alvis Owner Club meetings as she can, as well as planning a Continental tour. It was also used as the wedding car for her eldest daughter, increasing the memories of the car for her, her family and the next generation of Alvis enthusiasts.

After the start of World War I, John moved from shipbuilding into the nascent aviation industry, when he joined the Siddeley-Deasy Motor Company in 1915 as Works Manager and Chief Engineer. Based in Coventry, Siddeley-Deasy was engaged in the manufacture of the somewhat unsuccessful Puma straight-6 18-litre engine, which was used briefly by the Royal Flying Corps in the Airco DH9 single-engined bomber, where it was rapidly replaced with the Liberty V12 unit.

While he was at Siddeley-Deasy, John met Godfrey de Freville, who supplied aluminium pistons and casting for Siddeley-Deasy's aero engines, a meeting that would bear fruit in the near future. John had always wanted to be his own boss, so in 1919, at the age of thirty-nine, he set himself up in the engineering business by buying a small engineering company in Coventry, Holley Brothers Co. Ltd. He achieved this by using his savings and a loan from family and friends of £3,000. His first move was to rename the company T.G. John and Co. The company was based in Hertford Street in the centre of Coventry and was a general engineering works, serving the various manufacturers in the Coventry area, which included the makers of carburettor bodies for Zenith and the rights to build Hillman 4hp and single-cylinder and 7hp twin-cylinder stationary engines.

One of the first jobs that John started was to undertake the manufacture of a small scooter, the Stafford Mobile Pup, which was powered by a single-cylinder 140cc four-stroke ohv engine for Stafford Auto Scooters Ltd. However, John's aim was to become a manufacturer in his own right and the jobbing engineering work carried out by his company was simply a means to this end. His association with de Freville bore fruit in 1919, when he bought the rights to de Freville's design for a 1460cc 4-cylinder side-valve engine, along with the rights to the name 'Alvis'. This association was to result in the emergence of the first Alvis car, the 10/30, which was first listed in the T.G. John Ltd catalogue for 1920, where it featured as the '10-30 – The Light Car de Luxe'.

While T.G. John made the engine and many of the other mechanical parts of the 10/30, the chassis and body were bought in. The purchase of a new machine shop outside and to the west of the city centre on Holyhead Road was made in the middle of 1920, giving the company more capacity as production of the 10/30 started and by September production of the 10/30 was reported to number around five a week. John also purchased a foundry in Lincoln Street, Coventry, to the north of the city centre, where the Alvis tradition of making all its own aluminium castings was established – and of course it cut down the company's reliance on outside suppliers. Many of the workforce in the foundry came from the Royal Dockyard in Pembroke, with which John still had a close relationship due to his family and work connections with the area and he offered jobs to the Welsh locals when the Dockyard started to be run down in the

This early 'Winged Alvis' logo seen on a 10/30 model was changed to the 'Red Triangle' design in 1922, after complaints from Avro that it was too similar to their logo. The hare as a mascot was used on Alvis cars through the 1920s and 30s.

ABOVE: **Typical of the Alvis designs of the 1920s, Jonathan Huggett's 12/50 offered a decent sporting performance coupled with a four-door, four-seat body.**

The later Alvis Red Triangle logo is seen here on Jonathan Huggett's 1927 12/50, along with the 'Hare' mascot.

post-war years. This led to the main language of the foundry being Welsh for many years – luckily John was fluent! With the success of the 10/30 more room was needed to increase production and John was able to purchase a plot of land to the north-west of Coventry city centre, on the Holyhead Road opposite the new machine shop.

Towards the end of the year, in November 1920, Alvis took its first stand at the London Motor Show at Olympia and White City – there was a complementary bus service between the two sites. Alvis displayed two 10/30s with Morgan 'Zephyr' alloy two-seater bodies, a single Charlesworth bodied four-seater and a complete bare chassis. By this time, T.G. John had appointed R.E. Jones of Bond Street, London, as Alvis's distributors. R.E. Jones had subsidiaries in Exeter, Bristol, Cardiff and Swansea, giving Alvis cars a good spread throughout the south of the UK, and the company also owned the Morgan coachworks, which made the 'Zephyr' bodies for the 10/30.

The new Alvis factory was established on the Holyhead Road (now the A4114), just to the north-west of Coventry, on the south-west side of the road just before the existing railway bridge, on the opposite side of the road to the

Holyhead Road machine shop. The construction of a new factory on the site was quickly achieved and early in 1921 Alvis moved out of the Hertford Road premises and into the site that would be its home for the next seventy years.

With the move to the Holyhead Road site, John was able to start to execute his ambition to have all the manufacturing processes housed under one roof.

In December of 1921, the company name was changed from T.G. John Ltd to the Alvis Car and Engineering Company Limited, aligning the company firmly with its car-making future. At this time engine castings for the 10/30 and 11/40 started to have 'Alvis' cast in, either to replace the cast in 'T.G. John' lettering, or just adding it to the casting along with the 'T.G. John' lettering.

In 1922, John appointed Daimler's Assistant Works Manager, Captain George Thomas Smith-Clarke, as the Chief Engineer and Works Manager, and W.M. Dunn as Chief Designer. In these roles, Smith-Clarke would take on the technical side of the company, looking after the development and production of the cars, while Dunn took on the design side, leaving John to look after the financial and administrative side of the firm. At this time, Avro complained to

The 12/50 was powered by a peppy 4-cylinder ohv motor. This is the 1465cc unit fitted to Jonathan Huggett's 1927 12/50.

The 12/50 came with a selection of body styles. This is the 'Alvista' four-door saloon, with a lightweight fabric-coated body which helped to give the car a good and lively performance.

Alvis that the 'Winged Alvis' logo was too similar to Avro's well-established logo, so Alvis changed its logo to the now classic 'Red Triangle' version, which would see the company through to the end of its existence.

Also in 1922, Alvis flirted with the cycle car concept, producing a small number of 1096cc V-twin powered 'Buckingham' light cars. These cars were originally designed by Buckingham and modified by Alvis. Initially, Alvis expected to produce about twenty cars per week, but hostility towards the car from some senior Alvis personnel, who saw it as diluting the Alvis reputation for quality, combined with the emergence of the Austin Seven light car, proved fatal and production was stopped later in the year.

In 1923, while production of the 12/40 continued, Alvis introduced its first ohv engine, which powered the 10/30 Super Sports. Based on the 1460cc engine, this engine was the forerunner to the 12/40 series of engines. Very soon after came the announcement of the 10/30 Super Sports, followed by the model that would form the backbone of Alvis's success in the 1920s and 1930s, the 12/50. The com-

pany was further boosted by the success of the 12/50 driven by C.M. Harvey in the inaugural Junior Car Club (JCC) 200-mile race at Brooklands, with a second 12/50 coming eighth.

By 1924, half of the Alvis cars produced were powered by ohv engines, but while the company was increasing production it also had cash-flow problems and in June the Alvis Car and Engineering Company was placed into liquidation by creditors Cross & Ellis and Ransome & Marles – both coachbuilders who wanted payment for bodies supplied to Alvis. A stay of execution was granted and the board was rejigged to try to get the company on a firmer financial basis. With the creditors paid in cash or debentures against the company, Alvis came out of liquidation and production carried on into 1925 with the 12/40 and 12/50 models, although this would be the last year of production of the side-valve engines. Also in 1924, Alvis introduced the option of front brakes on its cars.

The majority of the factory's engineering efforts, however, were occupied by the design and development of the front-wheel drive (FWD) cars and the associated racing activities.

In 1926, front brakes became standard on all production cars and the first of the Alvis straight-8 grand prix engines were produced. The following year saw the introduction of the first of the Alvis 6-cylinder road car engines, an 1870cc unit mounted in the 14.75 model, which moved Alvis upmarket. 1928 saw the introduction of the front-wheel drive road cars, which in 4-cylinder guise were marketed alongside the rear-wheel drive 4- and 6-cylinder models.

The 6-cylinder engine grew in size in 1929 to become 2148cc and powered the Silver Eagle model. Production of the front-wheel drive cars was allowed to tail off so that the company could concentrate on the ever popular 4-cylinder cars and the upmarket 6s.

INTO THE 1930S, THROUGH THE GREAT DEPRESSION AND THE PRELUDE TO WAR

By 1930, the 6-cylinder cars were making a name for the marque and the front-wheel drive road cars had been discontinued, apart from a few development and racing 8-cylinder double overhead camshaft-engined cars. In 1931, Smith-Clarke was appointed a Director of the company while continuing in his engineering role, and in 1932 production of the 12/50 ended, being replaced in the line-up by the Firefly. The 6-cylinder cars were boosted by the introduction of the Speed 20, with its low and sleek lines that epitomized the post-depression 1930s. Car development was concentrated on the 6-cylinder models and culminated in the 4.3-litre models of the late 1930s, which accompanied a wide and rather confused range of models, from the Crested Eagle, the Silver Crest and the 3½-litre, along with the Speed 20 and Speed 25 models. Engine sizes for the 6-cylinder models varied from 2148cc through to 4387cc and most sizes in-between!

In the mid-1930s, John started to look at ways of expanding Alvis and chose to look at the production of aero engines and military vehicles. The reasons for this diversification were easy to see – the car industry was starting to be dominated by large companies capable of mass production, which was intruding into Alvis's traditional market space and resulting in orders for cars falling. Aero engines and military vehicles were made in much smaller batches and to much higher engineering and quality standards than mass-produced cars, so were better suited to Alvis's ethos of high-quality engineering.

Car production continued, but licence agreements were entered into with French aero-engine producer Gnome-

The first Alvis 6-cylinder car was the 14/75 of 1927, which started a line of cars that would carry Alvis through the 1930s in style.

Two contrasting 6-cylinder Alvis cars pictured at a club meet at a wet Newlands Corner in Surrey. Left is a 1930s 4.3-litre drophead coupé with flowing bodywork by Offord and right is a 1966 Three Litre.

The first of the Alvis 6-cylinder engines had cast-alloy crankcases and a separate cast-iron cylinder block and a cast-iron head. This layout was adopted on the pre-World War II 6-cylinder units; this is one of the first, a 14/75 engine.

Rhône in August 1935 and with Hungarian armoured vehicle designer Straussler in June 1936. In order to have the space for the new enterprises, building work for a new factory next to the existing Holyhead Road premises started in the middle of 1935 and was completed in 1936.

When Alvis's plans to produce its own Gnome-Rhône based aero engines did not materialize, the factory was turned over to contract work for various other manufacturers, including de Havilland and Rolls-Royce. Alvis's Straussler based armoured car and tank designs also had little take-up,

and while Alvis gained valuable experience in military vehicle design, it would not produce a successful military vehicle in any quantity until after World War II.

With the advent of World War II, the company turned its energies to defeating the enemy. Car production ceased and the whole of Alvis's capabilities were used to support the manufacture and refurbishment of military equipment, most notably with the production of de Havilland propeller assemblies and the manufacture and overhaul of Rolls-Royce aero engines, including Merlins for the Avro Lancaster.

CHAPTER TWO

ALVIS 4-CYLINDER CARS OF THE 1920s AND 1930s

INTRODUCTION

After Alvis had been established, the first cars that the company produced were aimed at the middle to upper section of the market. They were not lightweight stripped-down microcars or cycle cars; rather, they were 'proper' cars that had all the features and built-in quality of the larger established manufacturers' products, but were produced on a slightly smaller scale than the then market leaders. While still focusing on the quality end of the market, the cars that Alvis started producing were relatively economical to run and were aimed at the expanding market for personal mobility, which was growing steadily after the Great War, fuelled by the ambitions and aspirations of the swelling middle class.

In common with most UK manufacturers, many of the pre-war cars produced by Alvis had model names of the

Typical of an Alvis from the 1920s, Peter Huggett's 12/50 is a four-door fabric-bodied saloon.

ALVIS TYPE DESIGNATIONS

Type	Description	Date
Side-Valve Cars		1920–2
10/30	Open two-seater. Bodies by Morgan, Charlesworth	1920–2
10/30 'Ten'	Open two-seat tourer. Named Alvis 'Ten'	1923
11/40	Saloon or tourer bodies by Carbodies, Cross & Ellis	1921
TA 12/40	Saloon or tourer bodies by Carbodies, Cross & Ellis	1922–3
TB 12/40	Saloon or tourer bodies by Carbodies, Cross & Ellis	1922–3
TC 12/40	Saloon or tourer bodies by Carbodies, Cross & Ellis	1924
TD 12/40	Saloon or tourer bodies by Carbodies, Cross & Ellis	1924
SA 12/40	Short chassis Sports	
OHV 4-cylinder 12/50		1923–32
SA	Duck's back two-seater	1923
SB	Tourer body	1923
SC	Tourer	1924–5
TE	Open tourer	1926
TF	Two-seat beetle back	1926
SD	Two-seater sports	1927–9
TG	Alvista saloon	1927–9
TH	Four-seat tourer	1927–9
TJ	Two-door coupé	1930–2
TJ	Two-door saloon	1931
OHV 4-cylinder 12/60		1932
TK	Two-door saloon or two-seat open	1932
TL	Two-seat open beetle back or four-door tourer	1932
Firefly		1932–4
SA 11.9	Firefly 1496cc	1932
SB 11.9	Firefly 12 1496cc	1933–4
Firebird		1934–6
SA 13.22	Fourteen, 1842cc, all-synchro gearbox	1934–6
OHV 4-cylinder 12/70		1936–40
SB	Saloon and drophead coupé	1936–40
SC 13.22 Series II	Four-seater Sports Tourer	1936–40

type 10/30, which reflected the RAC Horsepower Formula used to calculate a car's power rating for tax purposes and the actual power that the car's engine produced. The RAC formula measured a notional power output using the engine bore and the number of cylinders – the formula was $(D \times D \times N)/2.5$, where 'D' is the bore in inches and 'N' is the number of cylinders. In the case of the side-valve 10/30, the engine was rated at 10.5hp, but actually produced 30bhp.

The pre-war Alvis range was impressive for its breadth – the number of models produced is quite bewildering to the uninitiated! Alvis had various ways of naming models, usually with ether the horsepower method outlined above (such as 12/50), or a name (such as Speed 20) to distinguish an individual model. A further two-letter 'Type' designation was used from the early 1920s to distinguish the different versions of each model, such as 'TA' or 'SB'. This all seems quite logical, until you realize that the Type designation can be used on more than one model, or indeed on more than one version

The 12/50 chassis could be fitted with bodies of many styles that were designed and built by various coachbuilders. This is a four-seat tourer from the early to mid-1920s. The solid 'artillery' style wheels were superseded by wires in around 1925–6.

of a single model. On top of this, the chassis could be fitted with bodies of various types from different coachbuilders. The table on page 21 seeks to bring some clarity to the puzzle and will hopefully enable an Alvis novice to work out what an individual model's designation actually means.

FIRST CARS – SIDE-VALVE 4-CYLINDER MODELS

Introduction to the 10/30 and the 11/40

The first car produced wholly by Alvis and badged with the Alvis name was a relatively small but upmarket car with initially a two-or four-seater open body, which was powered by Alvis's first engine. This was the 10/30, which was introduced to the public in March 1920 at the Scottish Motor Show.

Powered de Freville's 1460cc side-valve 4-cylinder unit, which was licensed for production by Alvis, and with an all-steel ladder chassis bought in from McNeil of Scotland

and two- or four-seat bodies, Alvis described it as 'the car for the Connoisseur' and priced it at £685, 'delivered from stock'. While the four-seat body was conventional, made with alloy panels over an ash frame, the two-seat body was a rakish open-topped style, supplied by the Morgan Company of Leighton Buzzard (not the better known Morgan Motor Company of Malvern). It was made of aluminium panels on a wire-braced, welded-steel tube frame, described by Morgan as the 'Zephyr' system. This, in principle, was not dissimilar to the Superleggera bodies produced later by the Italians and this method of construction resulted in a lightweight structure that contributed to the weight of the two-seat 10/30 being about 1,568lb (711kg), which gave the car a sparkling performance and started Alvis's reputation for producing well-engineered, sporting cars. Alvis stopped fitting Morgan bodies to the 10/30 in 1921.

Four-seater bodies were constructed by Charlesworth Ltd of Much Park Street in Coventry. Unfortunately, the four-seater bodies proved to be less popular than the sporting Morgan bodies, which meant that Charlesworth would not

The dicky seat on the 1922 10/30 sits behind the cockpit and is not covered by the hood when it was up.

see much business from Alvis until the 1930s, when the company produced the striking and popular bodies for the Speed 20 and subsequent models up to the start of World War II.

The 10/30 was followed by the 1598cc 11/40 in 1921, with its chassis supplied by Woodhead. The final side-valve car was the 12/40, introduced in 1922. Production of side-valve cars finished in 1924, when Alvis concentrated on the popular overhead-valve 12/50.

The Side-Valve 4-Cylinder Engine

The motive power for the new car came from a 1460cc in-line 4-cylinder engine, designed by de Freville and licensed to Alvis. The side-valve unit had a bore and stroke of 65 × 110mm, giving an RAC horsepower rating (for tax purposes) of 10, but which produced an actual claimed 30bhp at 3,500rpm – hence the name 10/30. The engine had a one-piece cast-iron combined cylinder block and head, which was bolted to a cast-alloy crankcase with separate cast-alloy sump. Early versions of the sump had cooling fins cast in, but

these were found to fill up with dirt and serve no useful purpose, so were discarded on later engines. The valves were accessed through screw-in caps on the top of the assembly, and the caps over the inlet valves also carried the spark plugs. The inlet valves were made from nickel steel and the exhaust valve from Tungsten steel. All eight valves were set in a line on the left-hand side of the engine and ran in phosphor bronze guides.

Cylinders one and four had their own exhaust ports on the side of the block, while the middle two cylinders shared a central exhaust port. Each of the two inlet ports were shared by two cylinders, with one passing between and feeding cylinders one and two, and the second between cylinders three and four. The valves were operated from the camshaft by rollers and the tappet clearance on the first seventy-five engines was adjusted using shims, then the design changed to give conventional screw and lock nut adjustment.

The valve operating mechanism was covered by a quickly detachable plate on the left-hand side of the engine. The crankshaft was made from 60ton nickel steel and was fully machined. The steel connecting rods were 'H' section for

The 10/30's 1460cc engine was a side-valve unit. The inlet manifold was on the right-hand side and was fed from an updraft carburettor. The fuel tank was mounted on the scuttle and the filler cap is visible on the top right.

The 10/30's exhaust exited on the left-hand side of the engine and beneath it is the cover giving access to the valve gear. Beneath that is the magneto. The cooling system was by thremosyphon, with no water pump. The large alloy water jacket on top of the cylinder head collected hot water from the engine and fed it to the top of the radiator.

The 10/30's cabin and instrument panel was simplicity itself. There was no attempt to style the interior – practicality was the norm.

lightness and strength, and the big ends were lined with white metal. Pistons were cast alloy with two piston rings. The gudgeon pins were floating and held in the piston by alloy end caps, and ran on plain phosphor bronze bearings. The crankshaft was supported in the crankcase on three white-metal plain main bearings and drove the camshaft via a train of three gears in a timing case at the front of the engine. The crankshaft and camshaft gears were of steel helical tooth form, while the central intermediate bearing was made from phosphor bronze. The camshaft was carried in the crankcase on phosphor bronze bushes and the end float was controlled using an adjuster bolt in the front of the timing case. The camshaft drive was used to drive the magneto, which could consist of a BTH, a Fellows or an ML unit, using a Simms coupling that was mounted externally on the left-hand side of the engine.

Oil was pumped around the engine by an external oil pump mounted on the nearside rear of the engine and driven from the camshaft via a skew gear and vertical shaft. Oil was sucked from the 1gal-capacity sump through a strainer, then fed through an external galley to the crankshaft and camshaft bearings through drillings in the crankcase. An oil-pressure

release valve was positioned on the rear of the engine on the offside; on early cars the big ends relied on splash for lubrication as the crankshaft was not drilled. The crankcase had cast-in troughs underneath the connecting rods, which had protrusions incorporated into them to act as dippers that threw the oil out of the trough and on to the big ends. The oil splash also lubricated the bores and small ends, with the oil draining down back into the sump by gravity. The excess oil diverted from the bearings by the oil-pressure relief valve passed into the oil filler on the rear nearside of the engine, which also acted as the engine breather. The filler also housed a gauze oil filter, which the owner's manual recommended should be cleaned every 200 miles to avoid it blocking the oil return. The sump was ribbed on all Alvis engines until 1924, when it was found that the ribs collected road dirt that prevented the ribs from acting as oil coolers.

The inlet and exhaust ports were cast into the cylinder block. The updraft Solex carburettor was bolted on to the block on the right-hand side of the engine, while the three-branch exhaust manifold was bolted to the block on the left-hand side. The inlet ports travelled from the valves across the block, where each pair of front and rear cylinders were combined and exited the block in a single point on the right-hand side. The exhaust ports were similarly paired, but the two ports exited the block on the left-hand side. Viewed from the side, the inlet manifold was 'T' shaped and the ends of the top of the 'T' were bolted on to the two ports on the right-hand side of the block. Low down alongside the block, the carburettor was bolted to the bottom of the 'T', where the charge had to travel up to the branch of the 'T' to get to the inlet ports. The exhaust manifold was on the offside and was a simple tubular affair with connections to the three exhaust ports, with the exhaust pipe exiting to the rear of the assembly.

The engine was cooled using a simple thermosyphon system, with no water pump. A large alloy water jacket was bolted to the top of the engine, which had a front feed to the top of the radiator. The hot water would circulate upwards into the top of the radiator. As it cooled, it would pass back into the block via a pipe from the bottom of the radiator that was connected to a port in the lower left-hand side of the block, behind the inlet manifold. Within the combined

cylinder block and head, Alvis paid a good deal of attention to the design of the cooling system, ensuring that the coolant passages were large enough to provide plenty of volume for the coolant between the cylinders and around the valve seats to eliminate any hot spots. Later cars incorporated additional plumbing to warm up the carburettor charge. An electric Bendix type starter and dynamo were mounted towards the rear of the motor on the left-hand side. The dynamo was mounted on the front left-hand side of the motor and was belt-driven from a pulley mounted at the front of the crankshaft.

The 10/30 Chassis and Running Gear

The 10/30 chassis was a basic ladder type made from 'U' and box section steel and comprised two longitudinal members joined by five transverse cross members, with springing provided to the solid front and rear axles by semi-elliptical leaf springs. The front beam axle was fitted under the chassis

Artillery wheels and no front brakes show that the 10/30 is an early car, but despite it being built at the dawn of the modern era, it is recognizably a motor car and has a performance that still makes it usable today.

on a pair of semi-elliptical leaf springs, which were mounted on the chassis longitudinally. To the rear of the chassis each longitudinal was raised over the rear axle, the front of each rear leaf spring was attached to a bracket on the longitudinal ahead of the axle, and the rear mount for each leaf spring fitted to the very end of each longitudinal with a shackle.

Pivot points on the chassis were fitted with supposedly maintenance-free oil-less bushes. The cast-alloy steering box was made by Alvis and was mounted on the right-hand longitudinal and was an alloy casting using worm gears to transmit the steering inputs to the wheels. The complete engine and gearbox assembly was mounted rigidly on a sub-frame, which was in turn flexibly mounted to the chassis. Power was transmitted to the gearbox by a leather-faced cone clutch and a short propshaft running from the engine. The gearbox was designed and built by Alvis and was a four-speed and reverse unit, which was unusual for the time and helped to give the cars their peppy performance. The gear-box housed two shafts and the gears in an alloy case and the shafts were supported on ball-bearing races. The gear change mechanism was housed on the top of the box, where it was connected to the gear lever gate, which was mounted on the outside of the chassis frame on the driver's right-hand side by an operating shaft. The live rear axle, again made by Alvis, was built from a cast-aluminium housing with straight tooth bevel gears and was connected to the gearbox output shaft by a steel propshaft, with a fabric universal joint at the front and a sliding spline at the rear. The 7gal (32ltr) fuel tank was sited under the scuttle and the dashboard housed a three-position tap – Off, Normal and Reserve, with the reserve being 1gal (4.54ltr).

With its lightweight two-seat body and good perfor-mance, the 10/30 got favourable reviews in the motoring press and made a neat, quality small car that attracted a discerning clientele, which was exactly what Alvis wanted. By carving out a niche in the upper levels of the emerg-ing market for motor cars with the 10/30, Alvis had placed itself in the profitable and sustainable position that it would occupy for the next four decades.

Development of the Side-Valve Cars

Production of the 10/30 was curtailed in 1921 when it was replaced by the 11/40 model. The main difference between the two models was the larger capacity of the 11/40's

The 12/40 with its overhead-valve engine replaced the 10/30 and had a performance boost as well. This pretty 1923 SB example is kitted out in a neat Carbodies four-door saloon body and is the oldest known surviving original saloon.

4-cylinder side-valve engine, which was achieved by increasing the bore from 65mm to 68mm, giving the engine a capacity of 1598cc. The modification retained the RAC tax rating of 11.4, as the rating was determined by the engine stroke, not capacity. The car was available with five body options: a four-seater tourer; a two-seater with a dicky seat; a closed coupé; an open four-seater with a folding hood; and a sports model with two seats plus a dicky seat whose distinguishing feature was a 'V' windscreen. The 12/40 was introduced in the middle of 1922 with touring coachwork and similar underpinning to the 11/40, although the propshaft gained a rear fabric universal joint.

The engine internals were modified to incorporate balance weights on the crankshaft and three piston rings, plus a new cylindrical oil filter was fitted that ran the length of the engine. The cooling system capacity was increased with the fitment of a header tank. The chassis was strengthened in 1924 to allow for the increased stresses of having four wheel brakes (an option introduced that year) and the supposedly maintenance-free bushes on the chassis were replaced with greased bearings. The 12/40 was to be the last of the Alvis side-valve family of cars as production finished in 1924, when Alvis concentrated on the popular overhead-valve 12/50.

PRE-WAR OVERHEAD-VALVE 4-CYLINDER MODELS – 12/50 AND 12/60

Introduction to the 10/30 Super Sports and 12/50

Despite the success of the side-valve models, it was obvious to Alvis that an overhead-valve version of its existing 4-cylinder engine was needed if Alvis was to maintain its position as a manufacturer of sporting cars. This resulted in the Alvis 10/30 Super Sports, which although fitted with a new overhead-valve head, retained the 65 × 110mm bore and stroke of the side-valve 1460cc engine used in the 10/30, rather than the 68 × 110mm 1598cc side-valve unit seen in the 11/40 and 12/40.

The 10/30 Super Sports and 12/50 Overhead-Valve Engines

Announced in June 1923, the new ohv 10/30 engine unit had a new cylinder head and separate cylinder block that was mated to what was in essence the side-valve cast-alloy

The 12/50 engine with its overhead valves produced more power than the 10/30 unit. Note the dynamo driven from the timing chest on the front of the engine and the magneto driven by shaft from the dynamo.

Pictured at an Alvis Owner Club meeting at Prescott circuit in 1973, this 1928 12/50 has a two-door sports saloon body by Carbodies.

The 12/50 engine had its inlet and exhaust manifolds on the right-hand side of the engine.

bottom end, with a three main-bearing nickel chrome steel crankshaft, steel connecting rods and alloy pistons housed in the large alloy casting. The cylinder block was in cast iron and was redesigned to incorporate a relatively large tunnel for the pushrods, which were equipped with springs to return them on to the cam followers. The tunnel was accessed via a rectangular alloy cover on the left-hand side of the engine, the opposite side to the inlet and exhaust ports. The inlet and exhaust manifolds were combined in a single complex casting that was bolted to the cylinder head and carried a single Solex carburettor.

The valves were placed in line in the head and were push-rod operated, with all eight individual rocker arms mounted on a single shaft. Oil was fed to the shaft via an external pipe from the crankcase and a restrictor screw was used to adjust the flow manually. Excess oil drained back down into the crankcase via a trough to lubricate the camshaft.

The new cylinder head was designed to have no water passages passing through the head gasket, removing at a stroke a common source of gasket failure on early engines, and a feature that would also be seen on Alvis's pre-war 6-cylinder engine. The cooling water was circulated from the cylinder block to the head via a cast-in water transfer port at the rear of the engine. This port proved to be troublesome to seal, so a detachable aluminium one was quickly introduced to replace it. Held in place by four studs, the detachable port was reliable and robust and solved the problem. There was no water pump and the thermosyphon system had cool water from the bottom of the radiator entering the front of the block, where it flowed to the rear of the cylinder block, up through the transfer port to the head and then to the top of the radiator, where the hot water was cooled.

Pictured at the Alvis Owner Club meet in 1973 at Prescott, this 1930 TG 12/50 is fitted with four-seat tourer coachwork.

The 10/30 Super Sports and 12/50 Cars

The 10/30 Super Sports used the older 110in (2,794mm) wheelbase chassis and it seems that very few were actually made, perhaps only the prototype, as some weeks after the announcement of the 10/30 Super Sports in the press, a second ohv model, the 12/50, was announced. This car was powered by a 1598cc ohv engine, based closely on the unit used in the 10/30 model, but with a bore and stroke of 68 × 110mm as seen in the 11/40 and 12/40 side-valve engines. The 12/50 initially utilized the 10/30's chassis and was first offered with a modified alloy duck's back sports body. As one of Alvis's most successful models, the 12/50 was offered in a number of configurations and bodies, with duck's back and four-seater touring bodies being listed during 1924. Model designations were many and varied, initially with 'T' used to identify touring chassis cars and 'S' to define sports models. The Alvista four-door saloon body was one of the most popular bodies that Alvis offered and was available for the 12/50 for most of its production life.

This was a fabric-bodied four-seater with four doors and a nicely appointed interior. It was a practical and relatively luxurious medium-sized car. The only downside was the lack of a boot, which was easily rectified with the fitting of a luggage rack on the rear end. The sports models designated 'SA' had 108.5in (2,756mm) wheelbases, while 'SB' cars had a 112.25 (2,851mm) wheelbase. The 12/50 was to become one of Alvis's most successful models and long-lasting, remaining in production up to the introduction of the Firefly model of 1932.

12/50 and 12/60 Development

The choice of engines used in the 12/50 changed in 1926, with the replacement of the 1598cc unit by the slightly larger 1645cc unit, which had a bore and stroke of 69 × 110mm. The chassis was also enhanced with a new design that replaced the previous unit's engine subframe with revised side members that were significantly deeper and stronger. The side members carried the six engine and three gearbox mounts, which were formed from conical rubber buffers and also allowed for wider coachwork to be fitted. The upsweep at the rear of the chassis was reduced to enable the rear floor of the coachwork to be flat.

All wheel brakes, originally introduced as an option in 1924, were now standard and were equipped with a single central adjuster as well as individual adjustment on each wheel. The brake drums were interchangeable across the car and the operation of the brakes was mechanical. Contemporary road tests found that the braking system performed well, with only moderate pressure on the brake pedal needed to bring the car to a halt. The four-speed gearbox of Alvis's own design and manufacture with a right-hand shift was retained from the previous model.

Cross & Ellis was another coachbuilder that produced bodies for Alvis chassis in the 1920s and 1930s. This is a 12/50 with coupé bodywork.

The Alvis designation system changed in 1926, with the introduction of 'TE' to define the touring chassis with the new 1645cc engine, and 'TF' used to identify cars with the sports chassis and 1496cc engines. In this guise, the 12/50 settled down for a long production run with only detail changes being made to the design. The 1496cc engine had its breathing improved in 1927, with the inlet ports being enlarged and a 40mm Solex carburettor, replacing the previous 32mm choke version and helping to pep up the performance. Known as the 'Big Port' engine, 12/50s equipped with this breathed-on engine and the sports chassis were designated 'SD' and guaranteed to lap Brooklands at 80mph (129km/h). Despite this improvement and being supplied in the touring chassis as the 'TH' model, the smaller engine was dropped from the range from 1930. For 1931, the 12/50 was offered with one touring chassis type, designated the 'TJ' and fitted with the 1645cc engine.

For 1931, the 12/50 was revamped to become the 'TJ' type and was one of three cars in the Alvis line-up, the others being the 6-cylinder Silver Eagle and the 4-cylinder 12/60.

The modifications made to the 12/50 were reasonably extensive. The engine gained a harmonic damper, as fitted to the 6-cylinder cars from 1927, which was mounted on the front of the crankshaft. Coil ignition was made standard, with the magneto becoming an option, while the one-piece manifold became a separate inlet and exhaust castings. The chassis was widened to give a 50in (1,270mm) track, which allowed for more interior space for the bodies. The petrol tank was moved from the bulkhead to the rear of the chassis.

The final version of the long-lived 12/50 came along in March 1931, the 'TK' sports version, which was quickly renamed the 12/60. The 12/60 was virtually identical to the 12/50, but had a modified manifold designed to take a pair of SU Constant Velocity carburettors. This gave a small power boost over the 12/50, with the gearbox ratios being altered to take advantage of the extra power. In 1932, the 12/60's sports credentials were further emphasized with a rev counter, knock-on hubs for the 20in wheels and a designation of 'TL'. The 12/50 and 12/60 were both replaced in August 1932 with the Firefly.

JONATHAN HUGGETT'S 12/50

Jonathan Huggett owns a number of Alvis cars, one of which is the most popular 1920s and 1930s model and the car that gave Alvis its reputation for producing sporting, lively and reliable cars that were a cut above the average – the 12/50.

Jonathan's is a 1927 Alvis TG 12/50 Alvista four-door saloon with fabric body by Cross & Ellis finished in Brown. The styling is unashamedly upright 1920s, with a prominent nickel-plated grille advertising its maker and a boxy saloon body with a luggage rack at the back to make up for the lack of an internal boot.

Driving the car is an experience, with its right-hand gear shift and non-synchro four-speed gearbox, but the perky 1645cc engine pulls well and gives the car enough performance to cope with today's traffic. Even the rod-operated brakes (luckily on this car operating on all four wheels) work well to shed any excess speed, although they do need to be adjusted regularly to maintain performance. When Jonathan bought the car it was fitted with some ancient Firestone tyres that were well past their best. Handling and grip have been improved enormously now that new modern but retro-looking Blockley tyres have been fitted, although the rear end is still a touch wayward in the wet.

Inside, the cabin is narrow, but there is enough room for a pair of six footers in the front, while the rear seats have massive amounts of legroom and headroom thanks to the long passenger compartment extending back behind the rear wheels. This is, of course, due to the car's lack of a boot, but the rear compartment certainly has enough room for a week's luggage for two.

Jonathan uses the car regularly, both for short and longer runs, and will often be seen at Alvis gatherings. On these jaunts, the car has a comfortable cruising speed of 50–55mph (80–90km/h). Probably one of Jonathan's best trips was taking the car from his base south of London down to Devon. The highlight of this trip was when the little car went to the Alvis South West meet down in Dorset, when it successfully climbed up the steep and treacherous hill at Tyneham View near East Lulworth, with Jonathan's wife beside him and the family dog in the back. Jonathan bought the car to experience the joys of owning and running a 1920s Alvis, with the car taking him back to a slower and more idyllic age and reminding him of the first time he travelled in a car – a pre-war Morris owned by his father.

With its narrow track and body and imposing radiator shell, Jonathan Huggett's 12/50 is unmistakably a car from the 1920s.

The interior of Jonathan Huggett's 12/50 is nicely patinated and largely original. The gear change on the right-hand side of the driver's seat can make quick entry and exits tricky.

Jonathan Huggett's 12/50 has no separate luggage boot in its Alvista fabric body, so a fold-down luggage rack is fitted at the rear.

With plenty of headroom and lots of window area, Jonathan Huggett's 12/50 is a nice place to be in. There is plenty of room in the back for passengers and the family dog.

PRE-WAR OVERHEAD-VALVE 4-CYLINDER MODELS – FIREFLY AND FIREBIRD

Introduction to the Firefly

After the success of the 12/50 throughout the 1920s , Alvis was fully aware of the importance of the model that had underpinned the success of the company and allowed it to go upmarket with the new 6-cylinder models. In 1931, The Motor magazine described the last of the 12/50 line as a car which was needed to 'meet the requirements of the large number of motorists who find it necessary to insist on low running costs and a relatively low annual tax, but who demand the characteristics of speed, ease of driving, and sturdiness which, of course, are prominent in Alvis productions'.

The 12/50 name was finally put to rest in August 1932 with the introduction of the Firefly. Powered by a heavily revised 4-cylinder engine with a capacity of 1496cc, the Firefly's roots were based on the running gear of the Speed 20. The Firefly's chassis was closely based on the 6-cylinder unit, albeit with smaller dimensions, and it fully exploited the design's lower centre of gravity. The engine shared its 100mm stoke with the 6-cylinder unit. The

The Firebird superseded the short-lived Firefly in 1934. This 1935 model with four-door saloon bodywork is powered by a 1842cc 4-cylinder engine.

The Firebird was Alvis's 4-cylinder model for most of the 1930s. With rakish looks, willing performance and a good price, it continued the Alvis tradition for small sporting cars. This is a 1936 model.

Firefly's engine kept the RAC rating of 12hp, as seen in the 12/50.

Supplied only with four-seat saloon or open tourer bodies, the Firefly was a welcome and up to date addition to the range, with its new engine producing a healthy 55bhp, up 5bhp and 10 per cent from the 12/50 unit. This helped to maintain the model's nippy performance, despite a 20 per cent increase in weight from the Alvista-bodied 12/50's 2,464lb (1,117.7kg) to 2,968lb (1,346.3kg).

Firefly and Firebird Development

The Firefly was relatively short lived, as it was replaced by the Firebird in 1934. The Firebird was a lightly revamped Firefly and came in three body types: closed four-door saloon; open four-door, four-seat tourer; or two-door drophead coupé. The main change was to the mechanical underpinnings, where the engine capacity was increased to 1842cc, with a bore and stoke of 73×110mm, giving it an RAC rating of 13.22. The new Alvis four-speed all-synchromesh gearbox was also fitted.

The engine incorporated a water pump in the front of the dynamo casing and the crankshaft was beefed up with bigger main and big-end bearings. Apart from the repositioning of the spare wheel from the rear of the boot to the left-hand side running board, the Firebird was virtually identical to the Firefly in appearance.

BELOW: **A factory picture of the 1935–6 Firebird shows the neat styling and rakish lines of this popular 4-cylinder model.**

Many Fireflys were converted into sporting specials when their saloon bodywork succumbed to rust. This sporting number owned by Owen Swinerd was spotted at an Alvis Owner Club meeting.

The Last Pre-War 4 – the 12/70

The last of the pre-war 4-cylinder cars was the 12/70. The car was designed to be simpler and hence cheaper to build than the Firebird and the main distinguishing mark of the model was the use of horizontal slats in the traditional Alvis radiator grille, rather than the vertical ones seen on the other models in the range. The car was powered by a brand-new 4-cylinder engine, designed by George Lanchester. Two notable points of the engine when comparing it to the existing 12/50 unit used in the Firebird was the positioning of the chain-driven timing gear at the front of the engine, the opposite to the 12/50 unit, and the use of a single casting for the crankcase and cylinder block. The engine retained the Firefly's bore and stroke of 73 × 100mm and a capacity of 1842cc, but unlike the 12/50 unit was of monobloc construction, with the crankcase and cylinder made from a single iron casting.

The final pre-World War II 4-cylinder Alvis was the 12/70. Based on the Firebird, it had an all-new 4-cylinder engine. Alvis's advertising of the time emphasized the sporting looks.

BELOW: **Introduced in 1936, the 12/70 body was designed to be simpler than the Firebird's and hence cheaper to make.**

The crankshaft ran in three steel-backed plain white main bearings and the connecting rods were forged steel, with the white-metal big-end bearings die-cast into the eyes. The pistons were in light alloy. The timing chain was a heavy duty triplex unit and the camshaft was positioned on the left-hand side of the monobloc, while the distributor was mounted on the right-hand side and was driven from the camshaft by a skew gear that ran across the width of the engine between cylinders two and three. The oil pump was submerged in the alloy sump and was driven from the lower end of the skewed distributor driveshaft. The alloy sump had a large gauze oil filter mounted on a bolted-on plate on its lower face.

The valves were placed in line in the head, which incorporated lozenge-shaped combustion chambers. The valves were held in place by dual concentric springs and the rocker gear was mounted on a shaft running the length of the head. Tappet adjustment was provided for on the tops of

The 12/70's engine was an all-new unit designed by engineer George Lancaster. With a bore and stroke of 73 × 100mm it had the same capacity of 1842cc as the Firebird's 12/50 based unit.

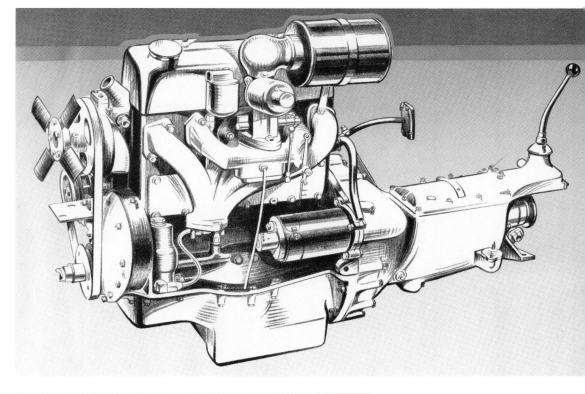

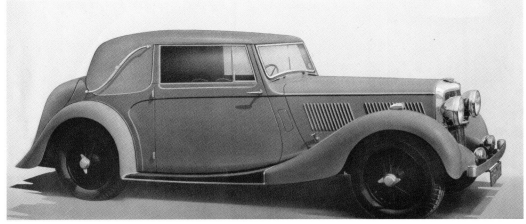

Like the Firefly before it, the 12/70 was also available in drophead coupé bodywork.

This 12/70 shows the Mulliners four-seat open tourer bodywork.

the pushrods, while the whole top of the head was covered with a neat alloy casting that carried the oil filler cap. The head had the spark plugs on the right-hand side and the inlet and exhaust ports on the left. The inlet ports were siamesed and, following 12/50 practice, the cylinder head to the monobloc face did not carry any water passages, with a bolt-on water passage mounted on the rear of the block and head and the top hose taken from a bolted-on casting on the front of the head, which also carried the water pump and cooling fan. The engine and gearbox were flexibly mounted to the chassis, with a single front mount, two mounts on the bell housing and a single mount at the rear of the gearbox.

The 12/70 chassis was a simple ladder type, with two longitudinals joined by cross sections. At the rear, the longitudinals were box-section steel and, from the rear wheels forward, were 'U' section to save weight and complexity. The front suspension used a beam axle again to save on complexity.

SPECIFICATION TABLE – 10/30, 12/50 AND FIREBIRD

	10/30 1922	12/50 1927 Alvista	12/70 1938 Saloon
Engine			
Type	Four-cylinder side valve	Four-cylinder OHV	Four-cylinder OHV
Crankcase	Cast alloy	Cast alloy	Cast iron
			One piece with block
Block	Cast iron	Cast iron	
	One piece with head		
Head		Cast iron	Cast iron
Cylinders	Four in line	Four in line	Four in line
Cooling	Water, thermosyphon	Water	Water
Bore and stroke	65 x 110mm	69 x 110mm	73 x 110mm
Capacity	1460cc	1645cc	1842cc
Valves	Two per cylinder	Two per cylinder, pushrod operated	Two per cylinder, pushrod operated
Compression ratio	4.3:1	5.35:1	6.3:1
Carburettor	Solex	Solex	SU
Max power	30bhp	50bhp	62.5bhp
Transmission			
Gearbox	Four-speed manual	Four-speed manual	Four-speed manual, all syncro
Clutch	Single plate	Single plate	Single plate
Suspension			
Front	Solid on leaf springs	Solid on leaf springs	Solid on leaf spings
Rear	Live axle on leaf springs	Solid on leaf springs	Solid on leaf spings
Wheels	Bolt-on artillery or wires	Wires Wires	
Brakes	Drums	Drums	Drums
Dimensions			
Track Front	50in (127cm)	49in (124.5cm)	50in (127cm)
Length	153in (389cm)	153in (389cm)	171in (434cm)
Wheelbase	110in (279cm)	112in (284cm)	106in (269cm)
Weight	1,568lb (711kg)	2,464lb (1,118kg)	2,576lb (1,168kg)
Performance			
Top speed	60mph (96km/h)	67mph (107km/h)	80mph (128km/h)

CHAPTER THREE

THE ALVIS FRONT-WHEEL DRIVE STORY

INTRODUCTION

While virtually ubiquitous on today's small and medium-sized cars, in the 1920s front-wheel drive (FWD) had only been experimented with in the USA and France, with mixed results. There had been no mass take-up by the major manufacturers, who preferred the simple and mechanically reliable front-engine rear-wheel drive format. One of the most notable experimenters was American Walter Christie, who would go on to limited fame as a designer of tank suspension seen in Russian BT and various British cruiser tanks of World War II, but his transverse-engined FWD designs produced in the early years of the twentieth century were not taken up by industry.

Post-World War I, American Ben F. Gregory patented his own FWD design and built FWD monsters powered by large-capacity Curtiss and Hispano-Suiza aero engines, which he used on the dirt-track races of the American mid-West. So Alvis was very much an innovator when it started to explore the use of FWD for general use in 1925. Alvis hoped to achieve a lighter weight by eliminating the prop-shaft and heavy back axle, and to obtain better road holding by giving the driver control over the direction of the driving wheels. Quite independently, Miller in the USA and Tracta in France came up with FWD designs for racing and sports cars, with similar aims in mind.

The Alvis FWD cars had an overhead camshaft 4-cylnder engine, seen here in a 1928 FE model.

The Alvis FWD road cars were made in the late 1920s. This is a 1928 Standard Supercharged FE model pictured in Red Triangle's showrooms.

FRONT-WHEEL DRIVE COMPETITION CARS

With the success of the 12/50, Alvis started to look at the prospect of entering the competition field to help with sales. As circuit racing in the UK was limited by law to the Brooklands circuit, the company decided to look at competing in sprints and hill climbs, as these were the only outlet for competition outside of the London-oriented Brooklands track. However, all public road-based compe-

titions, including sprints and hill climbs, were banned in 1925 following an accident that killed several spectators at the Kop Hill Climb.

Alvis started to support racing from the early 1920s, using cars based on the 12/50. Reducing the weight of the basic car was key, and in tuning the robust engine Alvis realized that it had a competitive car to race at Brooklands and also to compete across the country in sprints. The policy resulted in a famous win in the 1.5-litre class in the 1923 Classic International 200-Mile Race at Brooklands, in a 12/50-based racer driven by the works driver Major Maurice Harvey at an average speed of 93.29mph (150km/h).

Success in the 1924 season was to elude the Alvis 12/50. Despite the cars going through a major weight reduction programme and experiments with electrical-powered superchargers to up the power, it was obvious that the 12/50-based car was outclassed, in particular by the winning Darracqs and the AC's contender, which was significantly lighter and had a powerful 16-valve overhead-cam engine. This galvanized Alvis to embark on a major racing programme, with the intention of beating all comers in the 1925 season. In order to achieve this goal, Alvis realized that it would have to increase the engine power, cut down weight and make the car handle better.

The 1925 FWD Racers

Alvis was convinced that pulling the vehicle along with the front wheels rather than pushing it from the rear would give an advantage in cornering and traction, while the engine would have to be a derivative of the pushrod 12/50, with the power boosted by the fitment of a Roots type supercharger, and the chassis would be all new and built from lightweight aluminium. And so was born the first of Alvis's family of FWD cars, the 1925 racers, which were designed in two body types – one for Sprints and the other specifically for

the Brooklands 200-Mile Race. The Sprint Cars had low-slung bodywork, with a small fuel tank sited on top of the scuttle and a narrow and low-slung body with a rectangular radiator grille. The 200-Mile Race cars retained the low body and squat-looking radiator grille, but were fitted with a larger 25gal (113.7ltr) fuel tank on the scuttle and had a long, pointed tail. The cars were still powered by a 12/50-derived pushrod 4-cylinder unit, which was mounted back to front in the chassis. In front of the engine was bolted a large casting, which enclosed the clutch, the four-speed gearbox and the differential all laid out in a line. Fitted on each side of the differential unit were the two drum front brakes.

When fitted, the Roots type supercharger was bolted to the rear of the crankcase and was driven directly from the crankshaft. The chassis was a conventional ladder type, but was made from lightweight Duralumin aluminium alloy, with deep side members that were about 8in (203mm) in height. At the rear, the chassis was a semi-monocoque, with the seat, cockpit and bulkhead formed from several sheets of Duralumin, and a second sheet making up the rear of the cockpit and forming the back of the driver's seat. The front suspension was non-independent, with the axle formed by two tubular cross members running transversely across the front of the car, the ends of which angled rearwards to carry the wheel hubs on steering swivels. Four leading longitudinal quarter elliptical springs, an upper and a lower fitted to the

The FWD cars all had a large alloy casing bolted to the front of the engine to carry the transmission. This example has the gearbox positioned in front of the differential and output driveshaft mounts, the circular holes in the centre of the casting.

Viewed from the other side, the transmission casting shows the larger hole to allow fitment of the crown wheel in the differential section. Other versions had a different design, with the differential ahead of the gearbox.

The straight-8 dohc GP engine of 1927 had the transmission casting bolted on to the front.

chassis rails on each side, provided springing to the axle.

Drive was taken to the hub by shafts running from the differential, with universal joints at each end to allow for suspension and steering movement. The rear wheels were carried on a tubular axle and were sprung with reversed quarter elliptical leaf springs. The handling of the cars proved to be pretty good, but there were issues with instability under deceleration that got worse when braking heavily. This was due to the rear axle mounts giving insufficient resistance to the torque reaction when the rear brakes were operated, causing the rear axle to jump around and resulting in the rear wheels 'steering' and unsettling the car.

The cars enjoyed some success in sprints, and once they had been fitted with the supercharger Harvey gained a couple of international speed records. These records were both in Class F (for cars between 1100cc and 1500cc) and were the Standing Start Kilometre at 73.27mph (118km/h) and the Standing Start Mile at 80.84mph (130km/h). In September 1925, two cars were prepared for and entered for the 200-Mile Race at Brooklands, driven by Harvey and the Earl of Cottenham. While performing well initially, both failed to finish, one due to the front brakes overheating, which caused the differential bearing to dry out and fail, and the second due to over-revving while braking causing pushrod failure.

So while Alvis's experiments with front-wheel drive were not completely successful, the excellent handling characteristics of the cars gave the company the impetus and encouragement to continue development. For 1926, Alvis set its sights even higher with an assault on the pinnacle of international racing, by designing a car to compete in the 1926 Grand Prix class. The GP formula of 1922–5 had a 2-litre limit, which reduced to 1500cc for 1926 and 1927. Alvis had always been competing in the 1500cc class both commercially and in motor sport. In GP racing, Continental manufacturers such as Fiat, Talbot-Darracq and Peugeot had shown what small, high-speed engines could do and their technology was much more advanced, so this was a brave leap for Alvis to attempt.

The 1926 and 1927 Front-Wheel Drive Grand Prix Cars

To compete in the top rank of motorsport, Alvis knew that the straight-4 pushrod engine from the 12/50 would not be good enough, so an all-new engine was designed. This was a supercharged straight-8 unit with a bore and stroke of 55 × 78.75mm, giving a capacity of 1497cc. The top half of the engine, including the head, cylinder block and top half of

Seen here under restoration is the 1927 Alvis GP car. Note the 8-cylinder engine and the front-mounted gearbox. IAN MACKAY, BRADFORD UNIVERSITY

The 1927 car at an Alvis show in August 2014. The low stance is apparent, as is the delicate original paintwork on the remaining body panels. TONY COX

the crankcase, was cast as a single iron casting. The crankshaft was supported on five plain white-metal main bearings. Connecting rods were of cast Duralumin and the big ends ran directly on the crankshaft journals. A dry sump lubrication system was used with a gear type oil pump and separate oil tank to keep the engine's profile as low as possible.

The valves were placed horizontally in a row on each side of the top of the casting and were operated directly from a pair of high-mounted camshafts by rocker arms. A Roots type supercharger was driven off the rear of the crankshaft and in its initial form the engine produced around 110bhp. Alvis adopted a small diameter multi-plate clutch in place of the conventional 12/50 style of clutch. While the front and rear suspension of the new cars was the same as the 1925 cars, the chassis was made from steel channel and the semi-monocoque construction was abandoned in favour of a non-structural aluminium bodywork.

The fuel and oil tanks were carried low down beside the engine to keep the weight over the front wheels. The alloy bodyshell had room for two people – driver and mechanic, as the rules dictated, although the mechanic did not actually ride in the car. The rear end was a flat turtle back. Two cars were produced during 1926 and while the cars missed the British Grand Prix at Brooklands in August 1926, one, driven by Harvey, appeared at the Shelsley Walsh Hill Climb at the start of September and both were ready for the 200-Mile Race at Brooklands in late September, where they were driven by Harvey and the Earl of Cottenham. Unfortunately both failed to finish – Harvey was involved in an accident and Cottenham lost oil pressure and retired after running in fourth place.

The cars had held their own and were developed further over the winter, emerging with all new engines for the 1927 season. The engines retained the monobloc construction, while horizontal valves gave way to hemispherical combustion chambers with 45-degree inclined valves, operated from double overhead camshafts running in ball bearings. The unified iron casting included the head and cylinders.

The front end of the 1927 GP car shows its distinctive wide and low radiator. TONY COX

The crankcase was one deep casting, plus a bottom plate incorporating the oil pumps. The crankshaft was a built-up assembly using Baer patents, and used all roller bearings for the main bearings and needle rollers for the big ends.

The gearbox casting was completely redesigned so that the differential sat between the engine and the gearbox, which resulted in the gearbox being sited forward of the front wheels to improve weight distribution. One important consequence of this layout was that the driveshaft from the engine had to pass underneath the front axle shafts, which meant that the engine had to be set extremely low in the chassis. Although this was difficult to achieve, it had the additional benefit of giving an exceptionally low centre of gravity, making the car very stable in corners. The front suspension was changed to an independent system, using eight short transverse quarter elliptical springs, four on each side, with a pair above and below each driveshaft.

In 1927, the GP formula dropped the requirement for a second seat for a mechanic. Most manufacturers responded to this by adopting an 'offset single seater' configura-

tion, with the propshaft alongside the driver, and offset the engine and the rear crown wheel assemblies. However, for the FWD Alvis this was not necessary and Alvis's 1927 car was the first Grand Prix car to feature a central seat position for the driver. Two cars were built in this manner and one, driven by Harvey, was entered for the British Grand Prix at Brooklands on 1 October 1927, but engine failure in practice forced its retirement. Two cars were entered for the 200-Mile Race at Brooklands in the middle of October, driven by Harvey and George Duller, but again both cars retired with engine problems. This marked the end of Alvis's involvement in Grand Prix racing and dedicated designs for racing, but not the company's use of FWD cars in competition, as it embarked on producing FWD road cars with new overhead camshaft engines that proved suitable for racing in their own right. This was the final year of the 1500cc GP formula and the future of circuit racing was then uncertain, while road races such as Le Mans were becoming more important, which suited Alvis's aims of applying its FWD knowhow to road cars.

FRONT-WHEEL DRIVE ROAD CARS

Introduction to the Front-Wheel Drive Road Cars

While the company experimented with its FWD racing cars, it also was looking to produce a range of road cars that would complement the 4-cylinder 12/50 and 6-cylinder 14/75 rear-wheel drive cars and capitalize on the racing successes of the FWD drive cars – an early example of 'Win on Sunday, Sell on Monday' ethos.

To this end, Alvis's first front-wheel drive road car was the 1925 200-Mile Race car, rebadged as the '12/80' of 1926, a single example of which was offered for sale at the Scottish Motor Show with a claim of a maximum speed of 100mph and a price of £1,000. Although this model was also listed in Alvis's 1926 catalogue, nothing more was heard of it and it is thought that it was not sold. By 1928, production of a range of FWD cars was commenced, and these were fitted with either a long chassis with a 120in (3,048mm) wheelbase,

or a short chassis with a 102in (2,591mm) wheelbase. Both types of chassis were available with 4-cylinder overhead camshaft engines in normally aspirated or supercharged form, and from 1929 an 8-cylinder engine unit was offered as an option. The chassis was updated for the 1929 season by a redesign of the rear suspension and reinforcement of the chassis around the front axle and engine bay.

There were five versions of the front-wheel drive cars, designated FA to FE. The FA and the FD were short-chassis cars and would have been fitted with a two-seater body either of Le Mans type or TT type. The FD was fitted with the later modified chassis. The FB and FE were long-chassis cars and would have been fitted with four-seater open tourer or saloon bodies. The FE had the later modified chassis. The FC was the designation given to the six short-chassis works racers that were run in the 1928 Ulster Tourist Trophy race. While it does not seem to have been officially documented, the normally aspirated cars were generally known as the 12/50 (for example, the FA 12/50), while the supercharged cars were designated the 12/75, reflecting the increased power of the supercharged engine.

This FWD road car is a short chassis type fitted with sports two-seat boat-tail bodywork.

FRONT-WHEEL DRIVE ROAD CARS

FWD 12/80	Description	Date
FA	Short-chassis FWD two-seater body	1928–9
FB	Long-chassis FWD open tourer or saloon body	1928–9
FC	Short-chassis works racers	1928
FD	Short-chassis FWD two-seater body	1929
FE	Long-chassis FWD open tourer or saloon body	1929
8/15	8-cylinder dohc FWD	1939–40

The FWD road cars were fitted with this ohc 4-cylinder engine. The gear drive to the camshaft is on the front of the engine behind the flywheel and transmission.

The FWD road cars looked surprisingly 'normal' when compared to other cars of the day. This is an FE model from 1928.

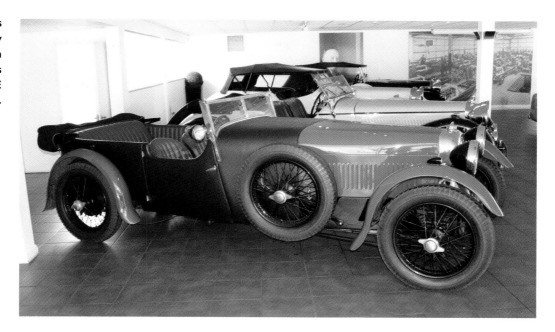

The mechanical layout of the FWD road cars was derived from the experience of the racing cars in the preceding years. The transmission layout with the gearbox in front of the engine and the differential at the front of the assembly along with the inboard front brakes was closely related to the 1925 race cars, while the independent front suspension was closely based on the 1927 race cars.

Engine

The 4-cylinder engine was an all-new overhead camshaft unit of 1481cc with a bore and stroke of 68 × 102mm. The engine's crankcase was a large alloy casting with a flat base plate. The crankcase carried 2gal (9ltr) of oil and in its base carried the oil pump and a long cylindrical suction oil filter, the front of which was fitted to the gear type oil pump and the rear to the pressure relief valve. Above the crankcase was a bolted on cast-iron cylinder block.

Three white-metal main bearings supported the crankshaft in the cast-aluminium crankcase and the connecting rods were in Duralumin, with the big ends in white metal. The crankshaft was drilled for pressure lubrication to the main and big-end bearings and splash from the big ends was used to lubricate the pistons in the bores. The light alloy pistons were fitted with two compression rings and one oil scraper. The overhead camshaft was driven by a train of

This close-up of one of Tony Cox's FWD restoration projects shows the view of the right-hand front of the engine and transmission. The inboard front brake drums are visible, as are the magneto and water pump, both driven from the timing gears.

noisy straight-cut gears placed in a timing case extending up the front of the engine. The camshaft itself had its own high-pressure oil feed, which fed oil through a hole bored in the camshaft to the camshaft lobes and bearings, which then drained back down into the sump through the timing case, lubricating the timing gears on the way down. The head itself was cast iron, had a solid copper head gasket and had the valves sited in a line along its length.

The camshaft operated the valves directly via buckets or dashpots fitted to the top of each valve and covered the dual valve springs that were fitted. The valves and their layout were identical to those used on the 12/50 engine. Valve adjustment was achieved using steel shims that were paced in a small cap fitted to the top of the valve stem to take up the clearance between the bucket and the camshaft. These shims were referred to as 'Hell's Confetti', a phrase that was coined by R.M.V. Sutton, a Brooklands driver who raced FWDs and also Aston Martins, both of which use Hell's Confetti. I don't think Sutton felt it was necessary to explain the name, as the shims were (and are) very fiddly things to handle, and adjustment was a nightmare because the shims have to be packed into a 'thimble' and when they are changed they never pack down quite the same. Also, they tend to settle and compress in use.

The camshaft was covered by an elegantly curved cast-alloy cover that was held in place by four nuts. The inlet and exhaust ports were on the left-hand side of the engine and the normally aspirated engines breathed through a 40mm MV type Solex updraft carburettor. Supercharged cars had the supercharger fitted on the left-hand side of the block below the inlet and exhaust manifolds and were powered by a shaft from the timing gear chest at the front of the engine and fed an MOHD type Solex carburettor.

In front of the timing gears was the flywheel and clutch (the clutch reverting to a design closely based on that of the 12/50) and the four-speed and reverse gearbox was mounted in front of this assembly. The four-speed and reverse gearbox was housed in a light alloy casting, with the casting including the bell housing and the differential, which was placed in front of the gearbox. The final-drive (crown wheel and pinion) gears were straight-cut bevels and hence noisy, adding to the engine noise produced by the timing gears. The output shafts from the differential carried the inboard front brakes on each side of the casing, which had ribbed cast-iron drums.

Chassis and Suspension

The front suspension was independent and the driveshafts were articulated at each end to form universal joints to allow for the suspension movement. At the outboard end,

The left-hand view of the front of the engine shows the supercharger fitted to the crankcase just below the exhaust manifold, as well as the differential casing just below the radiator.

The road cars had independent front suspension, with four transverse leaf springs.

the wheel hub was mounted in a spherical carrier that could swivel on kingpins above and below for steering purposes. This hub carrier was carried and partly enclosed in a split bearing housing, which was shackled to the ends of the transverse leaf springs. Dust and dirt were excluded from the spherical ball with felt seals. There were four transverse leaf springs on each side of the car and on all 4-cylinder road cars the leaves were clipped together using small coil springs to provide a damping effect, this being a method patented by Alvis. On later models, two Hartford type friction dampers were also fitted.

The rear suspension comprised a tubular leading arm, pivoted at the rear of the chassis, which was sprung with a quarter elliptical leaf spring running under it, with the front of the arm fitted to the front of the spring with a shackle. These springs also used the patented Alvis spring clips for damping, although on works team cars a friction damper was also fitted to the front of the assembly. This system was not a particularly successful design, leading to suspension wind-up and the leading arm would dig in and lift the back of the chassis upwards when the car was braked. The steel box-section chassis was a typical lightweight 1920s design and comprised two main longitudinal members joined with cross members. The stout rear cross-tube and a heavy cruciform

cross member provided stiffening against chassis twist. The fore and aft members were double height from the dash forward.

On the FA and FB cars, a substantial cast-alloy scuttle was fitted to the chassis above the central steel cross member. This helped to stiffen the chassis somewhat and the front cross member was bolted on in front of the engine and gearbox assembly. The front and rear brake drums were 9.4in (240mm) in diameter and were twin leading shoe on the front. Rear brakes were single leading shoe, this being conventional practice to provide acceptable braking in reverse or parked on hills. The wheels were the first fitted to an Alvis that used the Rudge-Whitworth splined knock-on system.

The front and rear brake drums had an internal diameter of 9.4in (240mm) and an outside diameter of 10in (250mm), including the cast in cooling fins. The front and rear brakes were rod operated and based on those used on the 1926 and 1927 GP cars.

Competition work with the FWD cars started with the works entering a pair of specially prepared normally aspirated fabric-bodied production cars into the June 1928 24 Hours of Le Mans race. The cars were driven by two teams, comprising Maurice Harvey and Harold Purdy sharing car No. 27, and Sammy Davis and Bill Urquhart-Dykes sharing

Rear suspension was a simple leading arm system with leaf springs.

The scuttle was a substantial alloy casting, which helped to stiffen the chassis and provided a firm mount for the controls and fuel tank.

The 1928 FE has a simple dash and cockpit typical of the 1920s.

The FE's 4-cylinder ohc engine is fitted with a supercharger. Bolted to the left-hand side of the crankcase, it offered a significant boost in power over the normally aspirated engine.

car No. 28. The Harvey and Purdy car came in sixth overall and won the 1.5-litre class, with the Davis and Urquhart-Dykes car coming in ninth overall. This was an outstanding result for Alvis, as it was the company's first attempt at Le Mans and the cars were a totally new design that justified the use of the road cars in competition. As a result, six cars were entered into the Ulster Tourist Trophy in August. These cars were based on the non-supercharged FA road cars and were designated the FC. Modifications included: strengthening fitted to the chassis in the engine bay; the cast footboard with its fuel tank support was replaced with an angle iron and timber fabrication; the steering box was repositioned and the steering column was modified to provide some adjustment; and a new, narrower all-metal body was fitted.

In the race, one of the cars driven by Leon Cushman came second, placed 13sec behind the winner. A few weeks later, Harvey took this car to compete in the Georges Boillot Cup in France, but engine problems forced his retirement. Harvey then used a specially built works front-wheel drive single-seat streamliner to take the 500 miles, 6 hours and 1,000 km Class F records at an average speed of 91.77mph (148km/h).

Alvis continued to market the FWD production cars through to 1929, but the market was not particularly enamoured with the cars and take-up was small. Alvis produced forty-three Le Mans and sixteen TT type two-seaters, thirty-five four-seat tourers, forty saloons and nine other chassis. This came to a total of 143 in all. Alvis ceased production of FWD road cars in 1929, but did produce ten straight-8 engined FWD sports cars, designated FA 8/15 into 1930, and one further advanced prototype FWD car with a 6-cylinder engine in 1931.

FWD Swan Song: The 1930 Straight-8s

Ten FA 8/15 8-cylinder cars were built during 1929 and 1930, and were used mainly for racing by the factory and for research into the FWD system. These cars were based on the road-going models, but were fitted with engines very similar to those of the 1927 Grand Prix cars. They had a reduced stroke of 78.5mm, giving a capacity of 1491cc, and were fitted with a built-up crank that used roller bearings for the main and big-end bearings, as well as steel connecting rods. Each valve was surrounded by a ring of

SPECIFICATION TABLE: FWD ROAD CAR

Engine

Type	Four cylinder overhead camshaft
Crankcase	Cast alloy
Block	Cast iron
Head	Cast iron
Cylinders	Four in line
Cooling	Water
Bore and stroke	68 x 102mm
Capacity	1481cc
Valves	2 per cylinder
Compression ratio	6.4:1
Carburettor	Single solex
Max power	50bhp (75bhp supercharged)

Transmission

Gearbox	Four-speed manual
Clutch	Single plate

Suspension

Front	Solid axle, four transverse leaf springs
Rear	Independent by leading arm, leaf springs

Brakes

Drums	
Type and size	Front TLS, rear SLS; both 9.4in (240mm) internal diameter

Dimensions

Track	54in (137.2cm)
Wheelbase	102in (259cm) or 120in (305cm)
Width	69in (175cm)
Weight (saloon body)	2,800lb (1,270kg)

Performance (no figures available)

THE TONY COX STORY

Tony Cox is probably the doyen of the FWD Alvis world. He is not only restoring a brace of 1928 FWD road cars, a short-chassis TD Replica and a long-chassis FB Carbodies four-seat tourer, he also runs the FWD section of the Alvis Register, is the webmaster of 'Hell's Confetti', the only website dedicated to the FWD cars, and last, but certainly not least, is the half-owner with Alan Stote of the only surviving Alvis straight-8 engined FWD Grand Prix car. When Tony and Alan bought the car they knew that it was an amalgam of various Alvis 8-cylinder parts, and although the chassis, bulkhead, bodyshell and front axle were all from the 1927 Grand Prix car, the engine and gearbox were a 1929/30 unit. The rear suspension was wrong and the chassis had been cut about to fit the later engine – although the damage was limited and relatively easily repairable.

Tony and Alan are in the process of restoring the car, which is proving to be a challenge – among other tasks they have had to recreate the 1927 engine and gearbox (or transaxle as it would be called today) to make the restoration as accurate as possible. They are aiming to reassemble the 1927 single-seater racer with as many

original parts as possible, plus accurate reproduction parts to replace the missing and unobtainable items. Once that project is completed, the later 1929/30 engine and gearbox will then form the basis for the construction of a 1929 FWD sports car, using as many original parts as possible, many of which are identical to the 4-cylinder equivalents.

Tony's expertise and knowledge of the FWD Alvis is probably unmatched; he has owned or part-owned five of them and has visited and inspected thirty-five out of the surviving forty cars, several being scattered around the world. As previously mentioned, Tony, along with Alan Stote, Tony's son Matthew and his friend Gerry Michelmore (another FWD expert), is currently involved in restoring four Alvis FWD cars, and if we bear in mind that there are only forty left in the world, these represent a significant proportion of the survivors. They are safe in Tony's hands; all the restorations are of a very high standard and when completed will be a credit to Tony's skills and care. It is the dedication of people like Tony who ensure that the heritage of firms like Alvis are still recognized and valued in today's throwaway society.

From the rear, the four-seat tourer bodywork of the FE does not give any clues to the technologically sophisticated mechanicals under the skin.

The quality of the work Tony Cox is carrying out on his restorations of his FWD cars is obvious from this close-up of the front suspension.

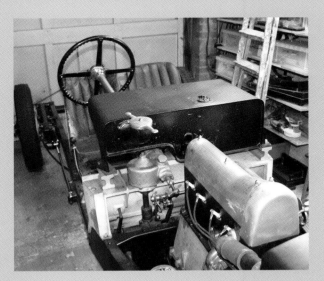

Tony's restoration project shows how the fuel tank is fitted to the top of the alloy scuttle.

nine small valve springs, an engineering solution to the relatively poor performance of single valve springs and a feature that would be seen on the later Speed 20. In this state the engines were claimed to run up to 6,000rpm and produce 125bhp.

The transmission unit was similar in principle to that of the 1927 GP car, having the gearbox in front of the axle, but the shaft layout was completely redesigned to increase the ground clearance under the engine, which was achieved by passing the driveshaft from the clutch over the top of the transverse axle instead of under it. The 1930 cars used magnesium alloys for the main gearbox and engine castings, resulting in a considerable weight saving.

The works team entered the cars in the 1929 Junior Car Club Double-Twelve race – a 24-hour race intended to rival Le Mans and held on 10 May, but run in two 12-hour heats, as Brooklands was not allowed to run races through the night. Mechanical problems meant they did not finish and the same happened at that year's Le Mans. However, a single-seater version did manage to get the Class F 1,000-mile record with an average speed of 95.24mph (153km/h). In 1930, Alvis entered four cars for the 1930 Ulster Tourist Trophy, driven by Maurice Harvey, Cyril Paul, Harold Purdy and Leon Cushman. Harvey had problems with brake adjustment, while Paul finished fourth, Purdy sixth and Cushman seventh, taking the first three places in the 1500cc class – a fitting tribute to the Alvis FWD cars and the last time they were entered in any competition by the works.

CHAPTER FOUR

PRE-WAR 6-CYLINDER MODELS

INTRODUCTION

With the 4-cylinder models selling well, the company introduced its first 6-cylinder model in September 1927. Given the Alvis type letters 'TA', the model had the designation '14/75', moving away from the old model numbering system of RAC rating/actual horsepower, as seen in models such as the 12/50. The new designation gave the exact RAC horsepower rating, 14.75, while not giving the actual engine power, which for the new engine was a healthy 61bhp. The new 14/75 was to be the sire of a range of cars that epitomized Alvis in the pre-war years – cars offering a combination of performance, smoothness, tractability, refinement and comfort that other manufacturers found hard to match. The range culminated in the Speed 25 and the Silver Crest models of the late 1930s.

PRE-WAR 6-CYLINDER ENGINE

The first of the pre-war 6-cylinder car engines had a bore and stroke of 63 × 100mm, giving a capacity of 1870cc, and the overall layout of the unit was used for all of the pre-war 6-cylinder engines. The crankcase was made of cast aluminium and had four plain main bearings to support the crankshaft. The gear type oil pump was submerged in the

PRE-WAR 6-CYLINDER CAR DESIGNATIONS

6-Cylinder Cars	Alvis Type Designations	Date
14/75	SA, TA and TB	1927–30
Silver Eagle	SA, SE, SF, SG, TA, TB, TC	1929–37
Speed 20	SA, SB, SC, SD	1931–7
Crested Eagle	TA, TB, TC, TD, TE, TF, TG, TJ, TK	1933–9
3½-litre	SA	1935–6
Silver Crest	TF, TH	1936–40
Speed 25, 4.3-litre	SB, SC	1936–40

ABOVE: **This 14/75 was photographed in Red Triangle's showrooms in 2017. It is a 1928 TA four-seat tourer with bodywork by James Young.**

The 6-cylinder engine was based on a cast-alloy crankcase, which formed the bottom end of the motor. This is an example in Red Triangle's stores and shows the three banks of 2-cylinder openings that allow for the four main bearings.

With its inlet and exhaust and manifolds on the left-hand side, the 14/75 engine set the format for the pre-war 6s. The exhaust exited forwards to cut down heat sink through the bulkhead.

substantial cast-alloy sump, which carried 22 pints (12.5ltr) of oil. The oil was fed through the crankcase, cylinder block and head to the crankshaft, pistons, bores and rocker gear through cast-in passages and drillings – there were no external oil lines. An oil filler was fitted at the rear of the left-hand side of the crankcase. A separate cast-iron cylinder block was bolted to the crankcase, and the cylinder head, also of cast-iron, was bolted to the cylinder block. The cylinder block was designed to ensure that all 6-cylinders had enough space for adequate water circulation around them. Water passages from the block to the head were external, with an alloy casting on the front of the head porting hot water to the top of the radiator.

The cylinder head was cast-iron and the valves were arranged in line with the rockers carried on a shaft running the length of the head. Oil was pressure-fed to the shaft to lubricate the rockers and the excess oil drained back down into the sump. All the inlet and exhaust ports were sited on the left-hand side of the head, with the six inlet ports siamesed (1 with 2, 3 with 4 and 5 with 6) to give three inlet tracts on the head. The inner exhaust ports were also siamesed (2 with 3 and 4 with 5), while the outer exhaust ports (1 and 6) were left as single outlets on the head, giving four exhaust tracts. The inlet manifold sat above and passed through the centre of the exhaust manifold to provide a hot spot for the charge from the single vertically mounted updraft 30mm Solex MOV carburettor fitted below the exhaust manifold. The exhaust

system was fitted to the front of the manifold to avoid heat soak into the cabin and was routed under the engine to the rear of the car. A cast-alloy rocker cover, secured with three nuts, covered the rocker gear.

The overhead valves were operated by pushrods from a camshaft in the left-hand side of the crankcase, which was positioned in an oil-filled trough for lubrication. The camshaft was driven from the crankshaft by a duplex chain, with the drive sprocket bolted directly to the end of the crank at the back of the engine. The timing chain also drove a second ancillary drive sprocket; this was used to drive the dynamo directly, which was fitted to the right-hand side of the engine. A shaft was carried forward from the dynamo to power a water pump, which was bolted to the block in front of the dynamo. In turn, a further shaft came from the water pump to turn the magneto, which was fitted to the block ahead of the pump. The timing chain drive was placed at the rear of the engine to be as near to the flywheel as possible and so eliminate any crankshaft whip, which would affect the timing. At the nose of the crank a torsional damper was fitted to reduce crankshaft whipping further; this was a common problem with many straight-6 or 8-cylinder engines of the time and if left unaddressed would result in the crankshaft snapping in two.

Pistons were aluminium and the connecting rods were made from Duralumin, with steel-backed cast-in white-metal plain bearings for the big ends and bushes in the small

With the spark plugs and ancillaries on the right-hand side of the engine, this 14/75 unit shows the cast-iron cylinder block and the dynamo, water pump and magneto and their driveshafts all bolted to the lower cast-alloy crankcase.

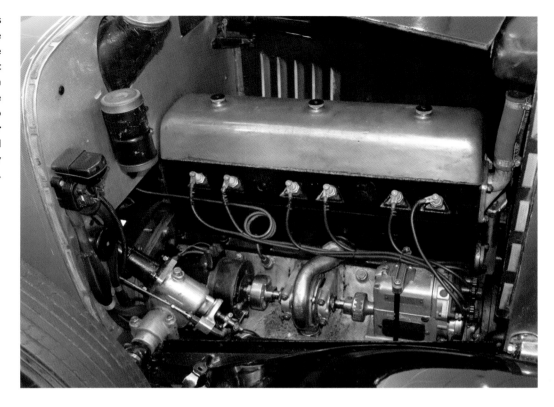

The mid-1930s Speed 20 6 had three SU carburettors each feeding two ports directly and a four-branch exhaust manifold. Note the alloy heat shield between the carburettors and the exhaust manifold, and the oil filler below the rear carburettor.

ends. The gudgeon pins were secured in the piston by either alloy end pads or circlips, and the valves were positioned vertically in the cast-iron head. The inlet and exhaust manifolds were positioned on the left-hand side of the unit with a single Solex updraft carburettor fitted, the opposite side to that seen on the 4-cylinder unit. The spark plugs, along with the magneto, dynamo and water pump, were sited on the right-hand side of the unit. While Alvis never released actual power figures for the 14/75 unit, various sources have estimated that the unit gave around 60–62bhp.

THE 1930S STRAIGHT-8 ENGINE

During 1934, Alvis designed a straight-8 ohv engine, which was aimed at enabling Alvis to compete directly with Rolls-Royce. The engines were fairly conventional, following the 6-cylinder design principles of an alloy crankcase and sump, a one-piece cast-iron cylinder block and a cast-iron head, but they featured 'cluster' valve springs. This unusual arrangement was intended to overcome weaknesses in the metallurgy of current spring manufacture and consisted of using eighteen small-diameter valve springs arranged radially around each valve, rather than a single or two springs fitted concentrically to the valve stem as is usual today. While this system did not appear to cause any problems, it must have been difficult to set up and assemble on a production line, but it was used on some of the later pre-war 6-cylinder production engines.

Two complete engines were produced and one was fitted into a 6-cylinder chassis, with a bespoke van bodywork fitted to disguise the car's origin. In use, the van proved to be pretty quick when compared (or unofficially raced on the public roads) with the competition. This vehicle was also used to test an experimental front suspension design that used rubber in compression for both springing and damping. While the suspension characteristics were found to be good, the fabric-reinforced rubber cylinders used instead of conventional coil springs were not robust enough and wore out rapidly, so the design was not adopted for production. A second engine was fitted to a conventional saloon body's chassis, but this unit suffered from a broken crankshaft early on in its life, which led to the development of the 8-cylinder engine being abandoned.

This basic design and construction was the same for all of Alvis's pre-war 6-cylinder engines, but as the engines grew in capacity, some engines gained additional main bearings and the bore and stroke were changed to give capacities that ranged from the original 1870cc with its bore and stroke of 63 × 100mm up to the mighty 4.3 unit with a capacity of 4487cc given by a bore and stroke of 92 × 110mm.

14/75

The first car to receive an Alvis 6-cylinder engine was the 14/75, which was introduced in 1927 and was fitted with the first variant of the all-new unit, with a bore and stroke of 63 × 100mm, giving a capacity of 1870cc. The 14/75 marked a significant move upmarket for Alvis, with its smooth 6-cylinder ohv power unit placing the car a class above the 12/50. The press at the time was impressed, with Motor magazine saying: 'As might be expected from a concern which has shown so much engineering skill and true pioneering work in the design of its cars, the new six-cylinder Alvis has many features of exceptional interest and is capable of an extremely good performance.'

The chassis and running gear were based on those used for the 12/50 4-cylinder model, with the same wheelbase and track (112in [2,845mm] and 50in [1,270mm]). The same range of bodywork was offered as for the 12/50, in saloon, tourer and sports forms. Due to the increased performance of the 14/75, four wheel brakes were fitted as standard – albeit still mechanically operated using rods. The brakes themselves were ribbed drums and the live rear axle and beam front suspension were suspended on semi-elliptical springs, which were encased in leather gaiters to hold the grease in and protect the springs from road dirt. The dash and bulkhead were a cast-aluminium structure, which was bolted to the front of the chassis and carried the 9gal (41ltr) fuel tank, with the filler cap accessed from under the bonnet. The name also marked a change from what had gone before, with the 14/75 representing the RAC power rating alone.

The flywheel was bolted to a flange on the back of the crankshaft-mounted timing sprocket and had a recess for a single-plate clutch. The clutch was initially fitted with the same nine-spring pressure plate as seen on the 12/50 unit; the number of springs was subsequently increased to twelve to cope with the 6-cylinder unit's increased power and torque.

The 14/75 interior is very similar to that of the 10/30, with simple functional design, minimal instrumentation and little effort put into styling.

By the 1930s, the Alvis 6-cylinder cars were pretty and sophisticated vehicles with a strong following. This is a 1936 Silver Eagle Type SG with four-door saloon bodywork.

ALVIS AND ITS COACHBUILDERS

The first Alvis car, the 10/30, had its chassis produced by Alvis and its bodies supplied by two coachbuilders. One coachbuilder was the Morgan Company of Leighton Buzzard, which supplied the car's two-seat sports bodies, made of aluminium panels on a wire-braced welded steel tube frame. The other coachbuilder was Charlesworth Ltd of Much Park Street in Coventry, which made the four-seater bodies. Alvis stopped fitting Morgan bodies to the 10/30 in 1921, and few of the four-seater Charlesworth bodies were supplied, but this initial production set the scene for Alvis's future car production – a system that provided great flexibility for the company during the 1920s and 1930s, but would lead to increasing difficulties after World War II.

Alvis had to find ways of getting a car to a customer. It could produce and sell a complete running and rolling chassis, for which the customer would then commission a coachbuilder to build a body, or Alvis could build a chassis that would be sent out from the Alvis plant to coachbuilders, who would construct a 'standard' body on the chassis, then return the complete car to Alvis for distribution to the customer. In the late 1930s, Alvis appointed a Body Engineer, one E.R. Fox, who oversaw the inspectors that Alvis employed to monitor body production at the various coachbuilders.

The only coachbuilder that could dictate its own prices was Vanden Plas. With an impeccable reputation for quality, a seriously discerning list of customers and a bulging order book, Vanden Plas could and did dictate its price to produce a body for all manufacturers (not just Alvis). Cars with Vanden Plas bodies from the pre- and early post-war years are still in demand today, despite the company's fall from grace in the 1960s, when it was lowered to the status of putting fake grilles, leather interiors and 'Vanden Plas' badges on a selection of British Leyland's small saloons.

The coachbuilding trade fell into a sharp decline after World War II. With the emergence of mass production, manufacturers switched from buying expensive labour-intensive wood-framed bodies to using steel bodies welded together from a relatively small number of large pressings that were mounted on conventional chassis.

From here, it was only a small step to dispense with the chassis completely and produce unitary or monocoque bodyshells, as seen today. The big manufacturers (such as Ford, Austin and Morris) tended to take the production of steel bodies in-house, starving the traditional builders of work, while smaller manufacturers (such as Standard-Triumph, Rover and Jaguar) outsourced the work of producing bodies to companies such as Pressed Steel, Carbodies and Mulliners of Birmingham, which had invested in the machine tools needed to press and weld large steel panels. Pressed Steel was eventually bought by BMC in 1965; Carbodies went to the BSA group, which

As war clouds loomed, Alvis continued to make some of its most attractive cars. This is a 1939 Speed 25 with a Vandan Plas sports body.

The 4.3-litre was the peak of Alvis's pre-war range. This side view of a drophead coupé shows the classic 1930s lines.

counted Daimler among its range of companies in 1954; and Mulliners of Birmingham was bought by Standard Triumph in 1958. The traditional coachbuilders could not compete on cost or speed of production, so were forced into a vicious spiral of having to move higher up the market, where production volumes were lower and eventually resulting in too little work to sustain their businesses.

The announcement by Rolls-Royce and Bentley that they would be producing their own pressed-steel construction bodies for their cars really meant the death knell for the majority of the independent coachworks in the UK. Alvis's last bodies were produced by Mulliner Park Ward, which was owned by Rolls-Royce. While this company made bespoke bodies to order for its parent company, the production of Graber style bodies for Alvis soaked up excess capacity in the workshops. But even this extra work could not save the company and Mulliner Park Ward eventually closed down.

Alvis's largest saloon was the 4.3-litre – this 1937 Mayfair Saloon is a fine example.

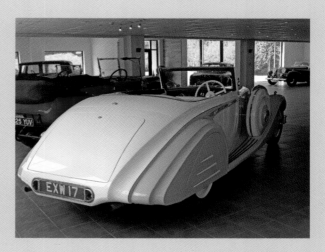

This Lancefield-bodied 3½-litre pictured in the Red Triangle showroom is a spectacular example of the late 1930s coachbuilder's art.

Alvis car production continued as the war started. This 1940 Speed 25 DHC is one of the last ones made.

The gearbox was a four-speed plus reverse unit, designed by Alvis and built and remotely located at the rear of the engine, connected to the clutch by a short Carden shaft. A tubular propshaft fitted with Alvis-designed roller-bearing universal joints at the end carried the drive to the live rear axle. This was made from an aluminium central casting containing nickel chrome steel bevel gears, which were case-hardened to promote longevity, and steel tubular outer arms carrying the drive-shafts and rear wheel hubs.

Unusually for the time, the electrical system was 12V. The chassis could be fitted with the patented Alvista fabric-covered two-door saloon body. Production of the 14/75 ended in 1930, when its place as the 'base' 6-cylinder model in the Alvis range was taken by the Silver Eagle.

SILVER EAGLE

The Silver Eagle was introduced in August 1929 as a higher performance version of the 14/75. While the engine retained most of the 14/75 unit's characteristics, it was bored out to 67.5mm, giving a capacity of 2148cc – the first of a series of capacity increases to the pre-war Alvis '6', which would eventually see it reach 4.3 litres. The standard model retained the single updraft Solex carburettor, but Alvis offered dual Solex carburettors as an option; however, the option did not prove popular as it appeared not to improve performance by much, if any, and increased fuel consumption. The Silver Eagle was offered in two chassis options – 112in (2,849mm) wheelbase, or 120in (3,048mm) wheelbase.

The Silver Eagle Sports model was introduced late in 1929 after the Silver Eagle was introduced. The revised engine was equipped with a new inlet manifold, which mounted triple SU carburettors. These modifications gave a power output of 72bhp, some 10bhp more than the 14/75, and endowed the new model with a significant performance increase. The increase in capacity meant that the model was designated 16.75hp, reflecting the RAC horsepower rating.

In 1930, the Silver Eagle chassis was modified to lower the whole car by around 2in (51mm). Coupled with a chassis which was shortened by 6in (152mm) within the wheelbase, the Silver Eagle went on to be produced up to 1937, and was the cornerstone of the Alvis 6-cylinder range.

SILVER CREST

Produced between 1936 and 1940, the Silver Crest was a cost-cutting exercise designed to produce a car that could be priced lower than the Silver Eagle. The design was the responsibility of George Lancaster and made extensive use of proprietary parts to reduce costs. The TF was powered by the 2362cc version of the Alvis 6-cylinder car and the TH had the larger 2762cc version. Both versions were popular and sold well, with the car only ceasing production in 1940.

SPEED 20

Probably Alvis's most popular product during the fraught years of the early 1930s was the Speed 20, which was first introduced in 1932. This model was a development of the Silver Eagle and with its 2.5-litre 6-cylinder engine and new style 'low-line' bodywork inspired by the 'SS' Jaguar models made possible by a new chassis, the Speed 20 had a combination of performance and looks that outshone all the competition. With its long bonnet fronted by a low-mounted but still impressive chromed radiator grille flanked by a pair of huge chromed headlamps, a rakish hood, flowing front and rear wings and a jauntily placed spare wheel on the nearside running board, the Speed 20 (and the later Speed 25), whether fitted with open-topped touring or closed saloon bodywork, was stylistically the epitome of the 1930s and, unlike some of the competition, had the performance to complement the looks.

At the heart of the Speed 20 was its chassis. While the layout of a pair of fore and aft longitudinals connected with cross members was broadly the same as that seen on the Silver Eagle and earlier Alvis models, the execution was different and would have a profound effect on the looks of the car. The front and rear of each longitudinal was swept up over the axle line, which enabled the centre of the chassis between the wheels to be lowered, while also reducing the centre of gravity of the rolling chassis. This was combined with a complex strong and rigid rear cross member, which was mounted inside of the anchoring points for the front of the rear spring and was higher than the side members, allowing it to support the body ahead of the rear axle. Constructed from 'U'-shaped channel-section steel, it had a central oval hole to allow the propshaft to pass through it and two triangular weight-saving cuts out of either side. This complex cross member was complemented by a tubular front member, conventional cross

The Alvis Speed 20 chassis was designed to lower the line of the car, with the front and rear longetudinals raised to enable a lower body line. This is a post-1933 chassis with independent front suspension.

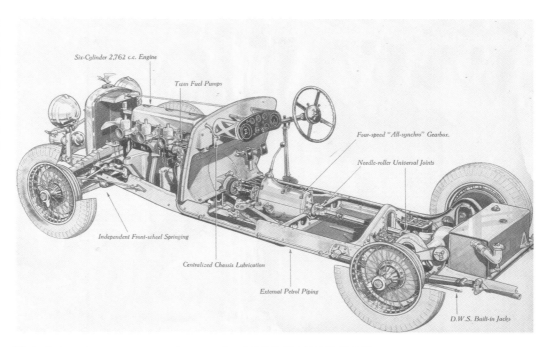

Six-Cylinder 2,762 c.c. Engine

Twin Fuel Pumps

Four-speed "All-synchro" Gearbox.

Needle-roller Universal Joints

Independent Front-wheel Springing

Centralized Chassis Lubrication

External Petrol Piping

D.W.S. Built-in Jacks

This 1935 Speed 20 with its striking DHC bodywork shows the low lines and impressive frontal view of the model.

members just behind the engine and radiator and a rear 'U'-section member connecting the rear end of the longitudinals, which combined to form a strong, light and rigid chassis. The car also sported a large rigid cast-aluminium scuttle, which effectively formed a bulkhead just behind the engine.

This contributed significantly to the stiffness of the chassis and carried the dashboard, foot pedals and assorted paraphernalia, such as the one-shot chassis lubrication pump and pedal, as well as various electrical components. It also formed a rigid base to which the bottom of the windscreen and the front of the body could be fixed. The front wheels were carried on a substantial 'H'-section forged beam, which was carried on a pair of longitudinal semi-elliptical leaf springs, as seen on the Silver Eagle. This

SPECIFICATION TABLE: 6-CYLINDER CARS 14/75, SPEED 25

	14-75	Speed 25
Engine		
Type	In line six cylinder	In line six cylinder
Crankcase	Cast alloy	Cast alloy
Block	Cast iron	Cast iron
Head	Cast iron	Cast iron
Cylinders	Six in line	Six in line
Cooling	Water	Water
Bore and stroke	63 x 100mm	83 x110mm
Capacity	1870cc	3571cc
Valves	Two per cylinder, pushrod operated	Two per cylinder, pushrod operated
Compression ratio	Not Known	6.1:1
Carburettor	Solex MOV 30mm	3 x SU
Max power	60 – 62bhp	106bhp
Transmission		
Gearbox	Four-speed manual	Four-speed manual all synchromesh
Clutch	Single plate	Single plate
Suspension		
Front	Solid axle, quarter-elliptic leaf spring.	Independent, lower wishbone, transverse leaf spring
Rear	Live axle, leaf springs	Live axle, leaf springs
Brakes		
Type and size	Ribbed drums	Ribbed drums
Dimensions		
Track	50in (127cm)	50in (127cm)
Wheelbase	112in (284.5cm)	124in (2855cm)
Weight (saloon body)	2,856lb (1,295kg)	4,088lb (1,854kg)
Performance		
Top speed	66mph (106km/h)	97mph (156km/h)

system was replaced with independent suspension in 1934. The lowered chassis side members meant that the body could be mounted lower than on the previous cars, resulting in a lowered stance, which gave the car a much more sporting look without compromising on headroom. The dampers were adjustable, using the André Telecontrol system, and allowed the driver to set the suspension to be anything between firm and sporty, to luxuriously soft as required.

The Speed 20 was powered by a 2511cc version of the 6-cylinder engine first seen on the 14/75, which, fitted with triple SU carburetors, had a power output of 85–90bhp. In RAC horsepower rating terms, the engine was rated at 19.82hp, hence the car being named the Speed 20.

CRESTED
EAGLE

The Luxury Crested Eagle complemented the sporting Speed models and was usually seen with limousine style bodywork. The chassis was a lengthened version of the Speed 20 and 25 unit.

CRESTED EAGLE

The Crested Eagle was produced from 1933 to 1939 and was aimed at the luxury market for saloons. The car's chassis was a lengthened version of the existing cars, with a 123in (3,124mm) and a 132in (3,353mm) wheelbase. The cars were fitted with the independent front suspension seen on the other 6-cylinder models, comprising a lower wishbone and the transvese leaf spring forming the top wishbone.

Various versions of the straight-6 engine were fitted, with capacities ranging from 2148cc, 2511cc, 2762cc and 3571cc. Usually fitted with four-door saloon bodies in four or six light forms, but also available with two-door drophead coupé bodies, the first Created Eagle came with a preselector gearbox, while the later version had the Alvis all-synchromesh box.

Alvis's independent suspension had a conventional lower wishbone and used the transverse leaf sprint as the top link. Hydraulically controlled friction type dampers were fitted which could be controlled from the driver's seat.

This 1933 Created Eagle four-seater two-door tourer was pictured at an Alvis Owners Club meeting at Prescott in 1973.

Later Alvis 6s had triple SU carburettors to give good power and torque. This shot of a car under restoration at Red Triangle shows the massive cast-alloy crankcase and the wide-spaced front-engine mounts.

Even with the hood up, this 1935 Crested Eagle four-seat, four-door tourer looks purposeful and the low lines are apparent.

3½-LITRE, SPEED 25 AND 4.3-LITRE

October 1935 saw Alvis announce the introduction of the 3½-litre model, one which was developed into the Speed 25 and 4.3-litre models that marked the peak of the interwar years for Alvis. Fitted with a development of the Speed 20's lowered chassis with independent front suspension, the 3½ was fitted with a new version of the Alvis 6-cylinder engine.

With a seven main-bearing crank, the engine had a bore and stoke of 83 × 110mm, giving a capacity of 3571cc. It was fitted with three SU carburettors to give a significant power boost over the smaller units. With the engine producing a claimed 110bhp, Alvis described it as a luxury car with the performance of a sports car and the car lived up to this

description. At the time, it was generally considered to be the best Alvis made. With a longer 126in (3,200mm) wheelbase, the chassis was designed to be fitted with saloon and drophead coupé bodies from various coachbuilders.

The Speed 25 was introduced in the autumn of 1937 as a replacement for the Speed 20. Using the engine, gearbox and suspension of the 3½-litre, the Speed 25 had a shortened chassis based on the Speed 20's 124in (3,150mm) unit, but had vacuum-assisted brakes and Luvax 'fingertip' controlled dampers rather than the Speed 20's André Telecontrol units. The Speed 25 was available either as a bare chassis for bespoke coachbuilders to body, or could be bought with a 'standard' four-door saloon or drophead coupé bodywork from Alvis dealers.

The 4.3 was introduced in 1937 and had a 4387cc engine with the same layout as the 3½-litre unit. The 4.3 was produced until 1940.

EDMUND WATERHOUSE'S SPEED 25

Edmund Waterhouse's 1937 Speed 25 SB saloon is the epitome of the late 1930s sports saloon.

With its low stance, flowing lines and rakish looks, the car gains admiring stares wherever it goes and so neatly sums up what was so good about the Alvis car of the 1930s. It is the sort of car that you imagine the upper-crust hero of the BBC's 1930s Paul Temple series would be driving with his glamorous wife Steve beside him on a fast lick out of 1930s London, as they chase down some dastardly villain that Scotland Yard has asked Temple to help apprehend. When I first saw the car swing into the Newlands Corner car park at an Alvis Club meet, I almost expected the 'Coronation Scott' theme tune of the radio series to burst out and for a debonair 1930s novelist and amateur detective to step out …

Edmund is pretty suave and debonair and as such the Alvis suits him down to the ground, with its fetching blue over silver paintwork. Edmund had run an excellent 1937 Lanchester 14 in his youth, which gave him a taste for pre-war cars and, some twenty-five years later, having the wherewithal to return to classic cars, he decided to run another pre-war car. Having done some research, he was drawn towards Alvis and, having joined the Alvis Owner Club, he found his Speed 25. When he bought the car he realized it would need some work, as it needed rewiring and the interior was somewhat tatty, then the clutch went! Not put off by this, Edmund set about getting the car into a presentable state.

One thing led to another (as they tend to in old car restoration) and the job turned into a fairly comprehensive restoration. Much of the ash frame of the body had to be repaired where possible and replaced where it was too far gone, and the bodywork was repainted from the scuttle back. The tatty interior was renewed and much of

Edmund Waterhouse's 1937 Speed 25 is exactly what a 1930s Sports Saloon should look like. The two-tone paintwork emphasizes the low and lithe lines. *(continued overleaf)*

(continued from previous page)

the interior woodwork was re-veneered and lacquered. Mechanically, the car was pretty good, with a new clutch and engine balancing being all that was needed, while the SU carburettors have recently been refurbished. While the work took some five years to complete, Edmund is more than happy with the quality and cost of the restoration, and now has a car that is swift, reliable and looks great.

On the road the car handles well, with precise if slightly heavy steering, and only a little wandering at higher speeds and minimal rolling when cornering. The car cruises happily at 50–60mph (80–97km/h), where it bowls along nicely on the flood of torque from the straight-6 motor; acceleration is brisk and effortless. In fact, for a car of its age the car is incredibly accomplished, and Edmund has to

remind himself that it sits on narrow Firestone tyres that do not offer the grip of modern day offerings.

Future plans for the car are clear. Edmund wants to keep it as close to standard as possible, preserving the car so that future generations can use it. The car has 78,000 miles (125,500km) on the clock, which appear to be genuine, and Edmund's next job is to reinstate the original Luvax shock absorbers, which are adjustable from the driver's seat.

And it is used – it gives Edmund a great deal of pleasure to drive the car and he has put a fair few miles on it. It is a regular at various Alvis Club meets and probably his best run was taking the back roads from Sussex to Welshpool for his niece's wedding. The bride stole the day, but the Speed 25 came a close second!

Edmund is really happy with his Speed 25. Used to indulge his passion for 1930s cars, the Alvis is driven frequently on both long and short trips and is a regular at Alvis Owner Club meets.

The Speed 25 interior is a lovely place to sit, with wood and leather in abundance. The steering wheel carries a knob that operates a hand throttle, ignition advance/retard and the lights.

Powered by the Alvis 6-cylinder engine, Edmund's Speed 25's engine bay shows many original features. Spare spark plugs are mounted on a neat holder on the bulkhead.

The rear seats in Edmund's Speed 25 are roomy and comfortable, with good access through the front hinged doors.

A sunny day and a rolling English road – I can't think of anywhere better to drive a Speed 25 like Edmund's.

CHAPTER FIVE

EARLY AERO ENGINES, ARMOURED EXPERIMENTS AND WORLD WAR II

ALVIS AERO ENGINES

Introduction to Aero Engines

With Alvis's approach to manufacturing resulting in minimal use of subcontractors and bought-in parts, the company was able to exercise rigorous quality control of the various components that made up the cars. This approach was of great significance when Alvis entered the aero-engine market, as it meant that the company could exercise the required levels of quality control which the safety-critical nature of aero-engine manufacture required.

The UK aero-engine market in the 1920s and 1930s was populated by a large number of small and not so small firms,

with the engineering (and car) firm Rolls-Royce producing engines alongside aircraft manufacturers such as Bristol, de Havilland and Armstrong Siddeley, which dominated the market for British military and civil aircraft. Smaller British players included Napier, Blackburn and Anzani, while European and American players included Germany's BMW, Daimler Benz, Hirth and Junkers, France's Potez, Gnome-Rhône and Lorraine, the Spanish-French Hispano-Suiza, Italy's Fiat, Piaggio and Alfa Romeo and America's Wright, Pratt & Whitney, Allison, Continental, Lycoming and Jacobs. This meant that there were a large number of players in what was becoming an important and growing market, especially as the world's democracies were starting to rearm in response to the threat from the rise of fascism. This gave rise to the

In the 1920s and 1930s, Britain produced a number of radial aero engines. Typical of these is this 450bhp 9-cylinder Bristol Jupiter, which was developed during World War I and was produced up to 1930.

72

Gnome-Rhône had a long history of producing aero engines, dating back to the dawn of flight. This Le Rhône 7-cylinder rotary engine powers the Shuttleworth's collection 1912 Blackburn Monoplane, the oldest airworthy British aircraft in the world.

prospect of increasing orders for military aircraft, although the larger industrialized countries favoured their own manufacturers for the production of military applications.

The First Alvis Aero Engines

The entry of Alvis into the aero-engine market was marked by two significant events. Firstly, Alvis entered into a licensing arrangement with French manufacturer Gnome-Rhône and in August 1935 Alvis spent £50,000 to buy the rights to build a range of radial engines based on the Gnome-Rhône 14L and 18L units. This, along with the recruitment of an ex-Gnome-Rhône engineer J. Pontremoli as Chief Engineer of the new venture, gave Alvis the product to enter the UK aero-engine market. The second string was the construction and fitting out of a factory to accommodate the new venture. The new factory was completed in July 1936 at a cost of some £87,000 and was built alongside the existing

factory on the Holyhead Road, but on the other side of the railway line that formed the north-western boundary of the original Alvis plant. The new plant was fully equipped with all new tooling and machine tools to produce aero engines. Alvis also acquired some further land at Baginton, then a suburb to the south of Coventry at the site of the new Coventry airfield, where an aero-engine test facility was built.

The original licence allowed for Alvis to take on the development and production of five engines, all of which were two-row radials. This started with the 14-cylinder Maeonides Major, which weighed 838lb (380kg), had a bore and stroke of 122 × 116mm and displaced 18.98 litres. The unit was expected to produce 700bhp, but did not make it off the drawing board. This was followed by a pair of 14-cylinder units with a bore and stroke of 146 × 165mm, displacing 38.67 litres. These weighed 1,250lb (567kg) and in Pelides form produced 1,103bhp at 12,000ft (3,660m), and in Pelides Major form produced 1,135bhp at 5,000ft (1,524 m). The final pair of engines had 18 cylinders, weighed 1,630lb

During the 1920s and 1930s, Gnome-Rhône produced many civil and military aero engines. This Farman F222 is powered by four Gnome-Rhône K14 radials, which were similar to the engine designs licensed to Alvis.

(739kg), and with a bore and stroke of 146 × 180mm and a displacement of 54.24 litres produced 1,375bhp at 13,000ft (3,962 m) in Alcides Major form and 1,502bhp at 5,000ft (1,524 m) as the Alcides.

Having gained the licence to produce the French engines in August 1935, Alvis then had to undertake a significant amount of work to anglicize the designs. The changes included: having to translate all of the annotations and notes on the engineering drawings from French into English; the substitution of English designed and constructed ancillaries such as magnetos and carburetors; the Continental specifications of the materials used had to be substituted with equivalent British specifications; and the metric screws, threads, studs and bearings all had to be converted to imperial equivalents. While this was a mammoth task, it was still less than designing a new engine from scratch and the first Alvis-produced engine, the 14L Pelides 14-cylinder radial, was first fired up during 1936 and had completed a 50-hour civil type test towards the end of 1937.

While this engine produced a healthy 1,065bhp, no manufacturing orders were forthcoming and only fifteen complete units were produced, which meant that the new factory was standing practically idle. Despite the lack of orders, in 1937 Alvis started designing its first all-Alvis engine, which was a smaller radial unit aimed at the 500hp market, slotting in below the Pelides. This engine would eventually emerge as the Leonides.

What the Pelides did achieve was to hone Alvis's aero-engine manufacturing and design skills and prove to the Air Ministry that the new Alvis plant was capable of meet-ing the strict quality controls and manufacturing standards that aero engines required. However, in 1938 the British Air Ministry informed Alvis that no British Government contracts would be placed for engines based on the French design. The actual reason for this decision is not known, although there are a number of theories as to the origin of the decision. These range from the political interference from other British aero-engine manufacturers to keep Alvis out of the aero-engine manufacturers' 'club', through to the fallout emanating from a number of royalty disputes between the French and British Governments, meaning that the British were opposed to any payment getting back to the French.

There were two sources of dispute over aero-engine royalties – the first dating back to World War I, with the French claiming that the British still owed them royalties due to the British manufacture of French Clerget-designed rotary engines, as well as for the incorporation of Clerget design elements in rotary engines designed and produced by Bentley. The second dispute was focused on the French avoiding the payment of claimed royalties to Britain, as the Gnome-Rhône company was originally licensed to produce Bristol Jupiter engines in the 1920s, but did not pay any on later Gnome-Rhône engines that Bristol claimed were direct developments of the Jupiter. On top of these theories, the issue of having a foreigner, namely Frenchman Monsieur Pontremoli, as the company's chief aero engineer did not endear Alvis to British officialdom, which saw him as a potential security threat.

The World War I vintage Sopwith Triplane was powered by a French Clerget rotary engine. The royalty dispute over the production and design licensing of these engines in the UK may have led to one reason why the Alvis Gnome-Rhône based engines did not make it into production.

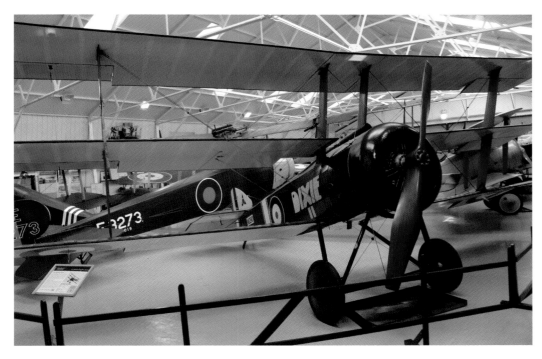

Subcontracted Aviation Work and a New Aero Engine

At a stroke, the British Military market was off limits to Alvis's new engine, so Alvis brought the licensing agreement with Gnome-Rhône to a mutually agreed end. Part of this agreement meant that for ten years (that is, up to 1948), Alvis would limit the capacity of any of its own aero engines to under 12000cc. This opened the way for Alvis to accelerate development of its new engine, which was a sub-12-litre radial aimed at the 500bhp market and which had no formal relationship with the previous Gnome-Rhône designs. The result was the Leonides, a 9-cylinder single-row radial engine that produced 450bhp and first ran during 1938, passing its 100-hour testing in August of that year.

The initial development of the Leonides was part-financed by the Air Ministry, which had at last given the company and its new factory the support and recognition it needed to be accepted as an aero-engine manufacturer. This new-found official acceptance led to the Alvis plant being able to start picking up Air Ministry work as Britain's industrial preparations for the inevitable war accelerated. The company's first contracts involved subcontract work for Rolls-Royce for aero-engine parts that Rolls did not have the capacity to meet. This at last gave the new plant plenty of work. At

Development of the first production Alvis aero engine, the 9-cylinder radial Leonides, was started during World War II.

the same time, the new plant was placed in the Government's 'shadow factory' programme, which was designed to disperse the production centres of essential wartime products, while increasing production capability by a significant amount to meet the needs of the rearmament programme.

With war clouds looming over Europe and production of all types of existing warplanes and their engines taking up all of the UK's manufacturing capacity, there was no room for a new design, so the development of the Leonides was temporarily halted. However, this did not mean that the new factory was idle. The subcontract work being carried out for Rolls-Royce was rapidly supplemented by more aero-engine related work for de Havilland and Vickers, plus orders directly from the Air Ministry for bomb-handling equipment.

At the outbreak of World War II in September 1939, all of Alvis's production capability was turned over to war work, but on 14 November 1940 the original Alvis car factory was bombed and destroyed by the Luftwaffe as part of the infamous Coventry Blitz. Many company employees were killed or injured, both in the factory and in their homes, many of which, sited close to the factory, were also destroyed. The intensity and accuracy of that night of raids has been well documented, as was the Luftwaffe's use of its 'X-Beam', or 'X-Gerät', radio-direction beams and receivers to establish the bombers' position and instruct them when to drop their loads. Luckily, the aero-engine plant only received minor damage. It seemed that the Luftwaffe's intelligence was not as good as their technical and pathfinding skills, as its maps did not show the new factory – only open space on that side of the railway, so the factory escaped being directly targeted.

Although the fabric of the original factory was wrecked, the company was able to recover a good proportion of the machine tools and equipment, which it then dispersed to a number of factories in the surrounding area, enabling Alvis to maintain production. The aero-engine factory was hit by the Luftwaffe in April 1941, which killed eight employees and badly damaged the tool room. By then, war work had been dispersed around the Coventry area and the company was able to continue with little interruption.

THE FIRST ALVIS MILITARY VEHICLES

Introduction to Alvis's 1930s Military Vehicles

As part of Alvis's desire to diversify and become less reliant on the car market, in the 1930s the company started to cast around for other related products that they could produce in their new factory on the north side of the railway. With Alvis's automotive experience, it was perhaps inevitable that the market for military vehicles was of interest, especially with the threat of war starting to emerge with the rise of Hitler and fascism in Germany and rearmament programmes being started in the UK and Allied countries.

The Straussler Connection

With the prospect of new markets for military vehicles being opened up by Britain's rearmament programme, Alvis cast around for a partner who could assist them to break into the market. One was found in the company owned by Hungar-

The chassis designed by Straussler for the first Alvis armoured car was a backbone design. With the engine in the rear and four-wheel drive, it defined the best layout for small armoured cars. PICTURE COURTESY OF THE TANK MUSEUM, BOVINGTON, UK

The prototype AC2 was sent out on trials to the Middle East by the RAF. Here it is in the desert as it was driven between Port Said in Egypt and Baghdad in Iraq. PICTURE COURTESY OF THE TANK MUSEUM, BOVINGTON, UK

ian Nicholas Straussler, who had developed designs for an armoured car and a tracked tank. In 1936, Alvis bought into Straussler's company and formed a new subsidiary, Alvis-Straussler Ltd, to merge Alvis's expertise in transmission and suspension design and Straussler's designs for complete vehicles.

Straussler's design of armoured car was at the time of interest to the Air Ministry, which had already commissioned a number of prototypes and tested them in the Middle East to assess their suitability for use by the RAF in their policing role in the various mandates held by Britain in that volatile area.

Straussler set up his UK-based company, Straussler Mechanisation Ltd, based in Brentford, North London, in 1933, and that year also saw him unveil the AC1 armoured car, a design was the first example of what would become the generic layout of purpose-built small armoured cars. While previous armoured cars were derivatives of cars or light trucks, the AC1 was a complete rethink of armoured car design, being unconstrained by proprietary layouts. This resulted in a vehicle with a rear-engined, four-wheel drive layout, with independent suspension all round using transverse leaf springs. The armoured body and suspension components were suspended from a steel tubular backbone chassis. There was a steering position at both ends of the body and the armoured body panels were bolted on to the chassis to help with maintenance. The car featured four-wheel drive and had a two-speed transfer box, which,

when coupled to the four-speed gearbox, gave eight forward and eight reverse gears. The independent suspension had a transverse leaf spring at each end and the drive system could be decoupled so that only one axle was driven. One unique feature was the provision of two steering positions, one facing the front and the other facing the rear, so that the car could be 'reversed' out of trouble if necessary.

The AC1's proposed armament was a .50 calibre Browning M.50 heavy machine gun mounted in the turret, along with an additional pair of 6.5mm (.30 in) Browning M.23 machine guns – one coaxial with the .50 calibre in the turret and a second that was carried in the car, which could be used in an anti-aircraft role from a mount behind the turret.

The AC1 was powered by a Ford 3.3 inlet over exhaust engine. The AC1 was tested by the British Mechanical Warfare Experimental Establishment (MWEE) based at Farnborough, Hants, but was found wanting; traction was not good and the vehicle would bog down and spin a wheel on 1:2 or steeper slopes. To counter the lack of power, Straussler tuned the Ford engine with a higher compression ratio, which meant that it had to run on high-octane fuel. While this appeared to fix the traction issues, the high-octane fuel required was not generally available to the military in the field, so the AC1 was rejected again.

The unsatisfactory AC1 was further developed to become the AC2. Two prototype rolling chassis were produced in Hungary by Weiss Manfred and one was then shipped to the UK. In 1935, one of these prototypes was trialled with some

The first production version of the Straussler armoured car was the AC3. This is the RAF version, with vertical side armour to give more room to the passenger compartment. PICTURE COURTESY OF THE TANK MUSEUM, BOVINGTON, UK

Another view of the RAF version of the AC3. These armoured cars were all deployed in the Middle East in the 1930s. PICTURE COURTESY OF THE TANK MUSEUM, BOVINGTON, UK

AC3Ds supplied to the Dutch East Indies had sloping sides, which improved the ballistic protection of the armour. This shot shows the wheel articulation achieved with the four-wheel drive and independent suspension. PICTURE COURTESY OF THE TANK MUSEUM, BOVINGTON, UK

success by the RAF in the Middle East, covering a route between Port Said in Egypt to Baghdad.

The final version of the armoured car, and the only version that made it into limited production, was the AC3, which was used by the RAF and other overseas armies, albeit in small numbers. The AC3 featured 9mm armour on the hull sides and rear, and 13mm on the front of the hull and the turret front, rear and sides. The hull featured vertical side armour between the wheels, giving more interior space, and the turret was manually operated. Retaining the AC2 four-wheel drive system with its two steering wheels, the AC3 was powered by a dry sump version of Alvis's 6-cylinder engine and had the same eight forward and reverse gears. It was 9ft 7in (2,921mm) long, 7ft 10in (2,388mm) high and 5ft 5in (1,651mm) width. It weighed around 5.9ton (5,994kg). In RAF service the AC3 was armed with a single .303 Vickers water cooled machine gun mounted in the turret. The car had a maximum range of 93 miles (150km) and a top speed of 48mph (77km/h). Twelve were produced for the RAF, designated 'Car, Armoured, Alvis-Straussler, Type A', and were all shipped to the Middle East for use as civil defence vehicles in the late 1930s.

Powered by an Alvis 6-cylinder engine and equipped with a four-speed gearbox and two-speed transfer box, the car had eight forward or reverse gears and could be steered from either end. The Netherlands ordered a further twelve for use in its colony of Java, now modern-day Indonesia; this design was designated the AC3D, with the 'D' standing for 'Dutch'. Straussler's design for the AC3D incorporated sloped side armour, with virtually no vertical faces on the design, predating the Russian T34 Tank, which is generally credited with introducing the sloped armour concept into service. Sloping the armour meant that the car's overall 9mm thick armour (although some sources quote 6mm) gave better ballistic protection than if it had been vertically mounted and also saved a significant amount of weight. However, even with the slope, the occupants were only protected from small arms fire or shrapnel from near misses, not from heavier weaponry. The AC3D was armed with two machine guns, one in the manually operated turret and the second mounted in the front of the hull. The final order for the AC3 came from Portugal, which ordered three AC3Ds to the same specification as the Dutch machines.

The Alvis-Straussler light tank was a small tracked vehicle designed by Straussler and the design was provided as part of the agreement with Alvis. The tank was quite small, measuring 15ft 6in (4,724mm) long, 8ft 3in (2,515mm) wide and 6ft 9in in height (2,057mm). Weighing 8.4ton (8,534kg), the tank was powered by a pair of Alvis 4.3 engines, each one of which drove one track though a fluid flywheel, and a Cotal electrically operated epicyclic gearbox, which gave eight forward and four reverse gears. Each track was supported by four wheels, the front and rear ones being large diameter and the inner two a smaller diameter. The wheels were suspended from cantilevered quarter-elliptical leaf springs. Unfortunately, the suspension was far too hard and had relatively short travel, making the machine very uncomfortable for the crew. In trials, the tracks were prone to being thrown when the tank was tilted and the testers were very wary of the impact that an engine failure could have on the tank's stability. The tank was rejected by the British Government and was not accepted by any of the potential customers.

Once the Alvis-Straussler subsidiary had been set up and a number of bays in the new aero-engine factory allocated to armoured vehicle production, Alvis set about producing the various orders. These included the twelve armoured cars for the Dutch East Indies, which were delivered in the late 1930s, and the three AC3D armoured cars for Portugal, which were delivered during 1937. In addition, a single tank was produced for Poland, which was unfortunately rejected by the customer in the late 1930s, and a number of tractor units and bomb trollies were produced for the Air Ministry. Orders for two tanks were commissioned for the Dutch, plus a further two were ordered by the Russians. However, none of the orders for the tanks were completed, as the design exhibited several flaws as described above, which made it unsuitable for service. During 1938, Straussler resigned and Alvis-Straussler Ltd was reorganized to become Alvis Mechanisation Ltd.

Back in Hungary, Straussler had entered into an agreement with the indigenous manufacturer Weiss Manfred Company in Csepel, Budapest, to produce for the Hungarian armed forces an armoured car that was closely based on the unsuccessful AC2. This new vehicle was named the 39M Csaba after the son of Attila the Hun. This small car had a turret-mounted 20mm cannon and a coaxial 8mm machine gun, as well as a second 8mm machine gun that was carried in the vehicle but could be mounted on the rear turret hatch in an anti-aircraft role. With four-wheel drive, a German Ford 3560cc 8-cylinder engine producing around 90hp and

The RAF AC3s were used exclusively in the Middle East. Note the water tank positioned inside the open side door and the Vickers .303 water-cooled machine gun in the turret. PICTURE COURTESY OF THE TANK MUSEUM, BOVINGTON, UK

9mm thick sloped armour, the vehicle weighed in at 5.95 metric tonnes. It was 14ft 8in (4,470mm) in length, 6ft 10in (2,083mm) in width and had a height of 7ft 4in (2,235mm) and had a maximum speed of 40mph (64km/h) and a range of 93 miles (150km). A second model, the 40M Csaba, was produced as a command vehicle. The 20mm cannon was removed and extra radio equipment and aerials were fitted. About 100 were manufactured in total during 1939 and 1940, and saw service during World War II with the Hungarian armed forces, which were part of the Axis forces supporting the Germans.

OTHER FIGHTING VEHICLES AND THE BOMB TROLLIES

Despite the international interest in the armoured cars, apart from the twelve cars ordered for the RAF the British Government did not award any further contracts to Alvis for series production and the excess capacity of the new factory was soaked up producing various items of equipment for the armed forces. Alvis Mechanisation produced a number of prototype fighting vehicles that were unsuccessful in gaining any UK contracts for their production. The first was an articulated four-wheel drive cross-country artillery towing tender, nicknamed the 'Hefty'. The second was des-

ignated the LAC for Light Armoured Car, and the third was a small, lightly armoured 'scout' car named the Dingo (not to be confused with the Daimler Dingo scout car that won the scout car competition).

The Hefty was an interesting vehicle with two axles, four-wheel drive and an articulation joint between the two axles. With the cab over the front axle and the load bay over the rear axle, the vehicle demonstrated excellent cross-country mobility, as the articulation meant that all four wheels could remain on the ground even in the roughest of terrain. Powered by a Ford V8 engine in the front half and based around a central tubular backbone, with solid front and rear axles, a prototype was completed in the late 1930s. While the design was not taken up by the War Ministry, the prototype was demonstrated to the Belgian Army, but no orders were forthcoming.

The LAC was designed as a Light Armoured Car, gun tractor or cross-country vehicle. The vehicle was powered by a pair of Ford V8 engines mounted side by side in the middle of the vehicle. Each engine had its own gearbox and drive system, which drove the two wheels on the same side. With independent suspension based on the system seen on the AC series of armoured cars with transverse leaf springs, the LAC was considered to have a good cross-country performance, but even with war looming no orders were forthcoming.

The Alvis Dingo scout car was a small four-wheel drive armoured car, which competed for a contract with the War Ministry. It was powered by a rear-mounted 12/70 engine. PICTURE COURTESY OF THE TANK MUSEUM, BOVINGTON, UK

The Alvis Dingo was a capable vehicle, but was unsuccessful in the competition to choose a new scout car for the Army. Here it shows its ability to cover rough and muddy ground. PICTURE COURTESY OF THE TANK MUSEUM, BOVINGTON, UK

Daimler's contender won the scout car competition and its car gained the 'Dingo' name. With the same layout as the Alvis car, the Daimler Dingo was a neat design that spawned a whole family of scout cars.

The Alvis Dingo was a small light reconnaissance vehicle that was powered by the new 12/70 4-cylinder engine. With four-wheel drive, a rear-mounted engine and a tubular backbone chassis, the design was again based on the AC armoured car. The rear of the car's crew compartment was open, armament was a single Bren Gun and the transmission had a transfer box to give four forward and four reverse gears.

When the car was tested during 1938 it performed well, with exceptional cross-country performance, but suffered from excessive engine wear. In competition with a number of other reconnaissance cars the Alvis lost out to Daimler's offering, despite it being lighter and cheaper. The Daimler offering went into production and the only trace remaining of the Alvis car was the name Dingo, which was adopted by Daimler for its scout car.

The final Alvis-designed product manufactured during World War II was a wide range of 'bomb trollies', essentially a series of four-wheeled trollies that were designed to move and handle bombs and other ordnance within an airfield or aircraft carrier. This involved supporting and securing the bombs while being towed behind a tractor or other vehicle. In some cases, predominantly for the Naval trollies used on aircraft carriers, hydraulic systems were incorporated to raise the ordnance to the level required to fix it to the aircraft. While not as glamorous as aero engines or armoured cars, the Alvis bomb trollies were a small but important contribution to the war effort and remained in production into the jet age. The trollies were made at the wartime Anstry plant and over 10,000 were produced during and after World War II in models that were capable of transporting and loading ordnance weighing up to 20,000lb (9,000kg).

WORLD WAR II – 1939 TO 1945

Alvis made a major contribution to the war effort mainly by supporting the existing aero-engine manufacturers. Work undertaken included: the production of numerous parts, including alloy castings, connecting rods and cylinder liners for Rolls-Royce Griffon, Merlin, Kestrel and Vulture engines; the production of parts for, and the assembly of, de Havilland variable pitch airscrews; production of over 10,000

During the war, Alvis was responsible for the manufacture and refurbishment of Merlin engines, as seen here fitted to a Hawker Hurricane.

bomb trolleys; and the production of spare parts for Lockheed undercarriage assemblies. Alvis also produced complete Rolls-Royce Kestrel and Merlin engines, which were used in the Miles Master trainer and the Vickers Wellington and Avro Lancaster bombers. Overhauls were undertaken of Merlin and Kestrel engines, and various major airframe assemblies were produced for the Vickers Wellington and Vickers Warwick aircraft, including control columns, engine controls and cannon mountings.

In order to have the space and resources to undertake the myriad activities that Alvis carried out during the war, the company took on the management and control of twenty-one 'shadow' factories to carry out the work. These were spread all over the country and ranged from taking over existing workshops and factories to new-build factories. These facilities were returned to their original owners or

disposed of after the war, with Alvis remaining in its Holyhead Road premises.

In late 1943, T.G. John, who had been suffering ill heath after working flat out since the start of the war, was ordered to take an extended rest period. He attended his final main board meeting early in 1944, when day to day running of the company was handed over to Smith-Clark. John finally retired later in 1944. A replacement for John as chairman was not made until 1946, when J.J. Parkes was appointed in January 1946. Following a period of declining health, John died aged sixty-six on 9 August 1946. With the war going in the Allies' favour in 1944, the Government allowed Alvis to commence planning for the peace. Initially, the company planned to produce 1,000 cars per year based on the pre-war 12/70, while it had also been awarded production contracts for the Leonides aero engine.

CHAPTER SIX

AFTER WORLD WAR II TO THE 1970s

INTRODUCTION

Post-World War II, Alvis had decisions to make and directions to follow if it was to remain competitive and successful in the newly peaceful but still troubled times. With three strings to its bow, cars, military vehicles and aero engines, Alvis had options and the company followed all three. In addition to these three areas, Alvis continued to make bomb trollies and was also contracted to produce printing presses designed by T.C. Thompson of Manchester. The Thompson-British Auto Platen Printing Press was used to print pages up to 10.25 × 15.25in (260 × 387mm), could print up to 4,500 impressions per hour and weighed around 3,360lb (1,524kg).

The press was produced by Alvis into the 1950s and formed a valuable additional string to the company's bow, while also assisting in the allocation of scarce resources in the early post-war years.

THE PEACE: 1945 TO 1966 AND BEYOND

One of the major issues facing all manufacturers in the UK after World War II was that the Government continued to control the allocation of steel. In order for a manufacturer to qualify for an allocation of steel, it either had to show that

EVENTS POST-WAR TO THE END OF ALVIS

Date	Event	Date	Event
Nov 1945	Leonides passes its 112-hour test run	1958	Park Ward takes over Graber body production
January 1946	T.G. John Retired in 1944 and replaced by J.J. Parkes	1966	Stalwart enters production
1946	Car production restarts with TA14	June 1965	Alvis agrees to friendly takeover by Rover
9 August 1946	T.G. John dies		
1947	Duncan Coupé produced	1967	Design of the FV100 family of tracked AFVs started
1947	Development of Saladin armoured car starts	1967	Last Alvis car, a TF21, produced
1950	TB14 sports car introduced	1968	Red Triangle set up to cater for spares and services for Alvis cars
1951	6-cylinder TA21 Introduced		
1951	Development contract for Leonides Major awarded	1971	FV100 Scorpion Light Tank enters production
1952	Saracen APC production started	July 1981	British Leyland sells Alvis Ltd to United Scientific Holdings
1952	Saladin armoured car production starts		
1957	Willowbrook-built Graber styled cars introduced	1999	Alvis Factory at Holyhead Road Site demolished

Alvis's first post-war car was the 4-cylinder 14, based closely on the 12/70.

a good proportion of the resulting goods would be exported to bring in desperately needed hard currency, or that the work it was doing was of national importance. In Alvis's case, this meant that it had to export the vast majority of cars it produced in the years after the war, but the steel supplies for the work on aero engines and fighting vehicles was not such a problem.

A second issue was the imposition of purchase tax on many goods. It was introduced in 1940 during World War II at a rate of 33$\frac{1}{3}$ on 'luxury' items and at one stage reached 100 per cent to encourage the populace to cut waste and redirect scarce resources to the war effort. At the end of the war, the tax was reset to 33$\frac{1}{3}$ per cent and was used as

a mechanism to help to control the economy. To this end, the rates were varied from budget to budget and in the early post-war years the rate of tax paid on cars was not only kept high to reduce demand and so allow more cars to be available for export, but was also doubled on any car costing more than £1,000, which gave manufacturers a major incentive to price their cars below that point. Later, the rate was changed according to the economic and Government spending needs, so varied between 20 per cent and 50 per cent. For example, in 1949, Alvis offered each of the three cars that made up its range, the TA14 saloon, the drophead coupé and the TB14 sports car, for £998 plus £278 purchase tax, just falling below the £1,000 cut-off for 'single' tax and

In the late 1940s, with problems finding coachbuilders to clothe the TD14, Alvis turned to Duncan to produce a small number of coupés based on the TD14 chassis.

In the early 1950s, Alvis introduced a new 6-cylinder car, the TA21. Here, a TA21 sits behind a vintage 12/50 from the 1920s.

The Graber-styled Three Litre was the final Alvis car to be made. This is Martin Slatford's TD21 Series 2.

The TD21 had modern lines and was a lovely grand touring car.

a rate of 28 per cent. In 1953, the Alvis Three Litre Saloon had a basic price of £1,250, then had £522 of purchase tax added – a punitive rate of some 42 per cent, meaning that the customer had to stump up £1,772.

These high rates of tax helped to damp down demand in the UK for new cars in the immediate post-war years when exports were all-important to recover reserves of foreign currency. Once the immediate post-war economic crisis had

been averted, the purchase tax rates, along with limitations on the money supply through hire-purchase agreements, were used for many years as crude market manipulators to manage the economy by driving demand up or down.

It was lucky, in this austere environment where raw materials were in short supply and demand for upmarket cars was variable, that Alvis had three strings to its bow, with the aero engines and military vehicle manufacturing along-

The TD's 6-cylinder engine featured overhead valves operated by pushrods and produced respectable rather than spectacular power levels.

side the cars. In fact, the cars were increasingly taking a background role behind the military contracts, with much of the factory's overall output dedicated to the Leonides aero engines and the Saladin family of armoured vehicles.

By 1946, Alvis had a full order book for the newly announced Fourteen, orders were starting to come in for the Leonides engines and discussions with the Government were in progress over the design of what would become the Saladin armoured car. However, problems with the supply of bodies was limiting production of the Fourteen, an issue that would dog Alvis car production for most of the post-war period. Design of the new 3-litre engine and the car to put it into had also started and the outlook for the company was good. However, the proportion of car-related work that the company undertook was starting to decline when compared with the aero-engine and military vehicle work. The seed had been sown for Alvis to bow out of car production, even as it was embarking on the design of a new car for the post-war age.

The car market of the 1950s and into the 1960s was characterized by the merging of most small and medium volume manufacturers to form larger conglomerates, which could cut costs by building fewer model ranges in greater numbers. Alvis's target market of medium-sized luxury but sporting cars was being squeezed at the top end by sports car manufacturers Aston Martin and luxury car makers Rolls-Royce, while the upper ranks of the mass-production companies, such as Rover, Triumph and Jaguar, were nibbling away from the lower end of the market.

In addition to the decline of the car market, with the advent of the jet age the piston aero-engine business was also in decline, with production of the Leonides aero engines halted in 1965. In the same year, Alvis was bought by Rover, which meant that the company lost its independence and then in 1967 it became part of the British Leyland conglomerate. Car production was quickly reduced and the last true Alvis car rolled out in 1967. Rover had made some half-hearted attempts to revive the Alvis name, but the efforts

The Stalwart amphibious load carrier was the last of the six-wheeled military vehicle line, entering service in the mid-1960s.

The Scorpion was the first of the FV100 family of tracked AFVs to enter service in the 1970s.

The last car produced by Alvis was this 1967 TF21, currently owned by Adam Gilchrist.

were quickly swamped by the morass of British Leyland and its struggle to survive.

This was not quite the end for Alvis, as a contract for the design and production of the FV100 family of Armoured Fighting Vehicles (AFVs) was awarded in 1967; production of these vehicles would start in 1971. So Alvis became the AFV element of British Leyland, but as a non-core part of a car manufacturer it was vulnerable and was eventually sold off to United Scientific Holdings in 1981. The buyer adopted the Alvis name to become Alvis plc.

In September 1998, Alvis plc bought GKN's AFV business and the business was moved to the GKN plant in Telford. The Holyhead works, and hence the last link with the original Alvis company, was sold off and demolished in 1999, to be replaced by a shopping centre – the Alvis Retail Park. Alvis plc bought Vickers Defence Systems in 2002, forming Alvis Vickers Ltd, which in turn was bought by BAE Systems in 2004. With this takeover, the famous Alvis logo finally disappeared, as BAE integrated Alvis Vickers into its own branding.

CHAPTER SEVEN

POST-WAR 4-CYLINDER CARS

INTRODUCTION

Compared to the vast and complex range of cars produced by the factory after World War I, the post-World War II picture for Alvis was a lot simpler, as were the model designations. Post-war Britain was in a dire state, almost bankrupt from the expense of fighting. The country was also suffering from worn-out tooling in tired factories and an infrastructure that had been flogged half to death to produce the weapons needed to win the war. Exports became a priority to bring in desperately needed foreign currency, especially US Dollars, so Alvis had to get a car back into production as soon as possible as the wartime contracts were rapidly cancelled. The answer, which was the same as adopted by most of the UK's car manufacturers, was to resurrect a pre-war model, dust it down, do a few updates and present it to the transport hungry masses as a new model.

Thus was born the first of the post-World War II Alvis family – the Fourteen (Type TA14), which was largely based on the running gear of the 12/70 of the late 1930s and was powered by the 12/70's 4-cylinder engine. The Fourteen got the company back into the car market and it compared favourably with the other early post-war cars, but with its 4-cylinder engine it was not viewed as being in the upper echelons of the market. To address this, Alvis needed an up to date 6-cylinder engine – the existing pre-war 6-cylinder design was showing its age, mainly in the design, which, with its separate alloy crankcase and bolted-on cast-iron block, was firmly rooted in the 1920s and 1930s. While it produced a healthy amount of power and torque, a replacement was needed and Alvis set about the design of an all-new 3-litre 6-cylinder engine, which followed contemporary practice in having a one-piece crankcase and cylinder block and a separate cast-iron head. This engine would go on to power all of the Alvis cars produced from 1951 through to the end of car production in 1967.

POST-WAR 4-CYLINDER CARS

Type	Description	Date
TA14	Upright four-door saloon body by Mulliners and DHC by Tickford and Carbodies	1946–50
TB14	Rakish two-seat bodywork on shortened TA chassis	1950
Duncan Coupé	TA14 chassis, Duncan pillar-less coupé bodywork	1947–8

THE POST-WAR 4-CYLINDER CARS

After World War II, Alvis needed to get a car into production as quickly as possible in order to meet the pent-up demand for new cars. However, this was not as easy as it seemed for several reasons.

Firstly, the post-war Government had imposed a number of fairly draconian rules on industry that affected all car manufacturers, but especially in the upper levels of the market. The first was the allocation of steel – priority was given to those companies which could demonstrate that the steel was used to produce goods for export, which would bring much needed hard currency into Britain. The second reason was the imposition of high rates of purchase tax on cars, which were doubled if the car cast more than £1,000. Thirdly, the bombing of the Alvis factory in 1940 had resulted in

The TA14 – Alvis's first post-war car. Available as a four-door saloon as shown here or a two door drophead coupé, it was powered by a 4-cylinder engine developed from the 12/70 unit.

This TA14 saloon photographed in the 1960s shows the separate headlights and early post-war styling.

The TA14's 4-cylinder engine had the traditional Alvis alloy rocker cover held on by wing nuts. A conventional belt-driven dynamo provided power and the distributor was driven internally from the camshaft.

the loss of tools, patterns, drawings and stocks of parts, all of which were needed if a car was to be produced quickly.

The good news was that Alvis had a reasonably modern engine, the 4-cylinder unit designed by George Lanchester. This was first seen in the 12/70 of 1936 and at under 2 litres in capacity would, in the right car, offer reasonable fuel economy and performance in keeping with the period of austerity. The car was always seen as a stopgap, as Alvis was already working on a new 6-cylinder engine to take the company into the 1950s. During World War II, Alvis had continued to advertise its intention to return to car building when hostilities ceased and this had generated a good degree of interest, so it was imperative to get a new model out in the market as soon as possible. Once the stopgap TA14 was in production, Alvis knew that it would have to create and produce a more modern design, rather than depend on what was obviously a rehash of a pre-war car, so the company was already planning a two-car range. This was expected to comprise 2-litre 4-cylinder and 3-litre 6-cylinder powered cars, with as much running gear in common as possible. However, in the immediate post-war years the TA14 was the best the company could do.

The TA14 – A Saloon for (Some of) the People

The TA14 was typical of the early post-war cars produced by most British manufacturers. As a light revamp of the 12/70, the car was a thoroughly conventional if somewhat dated take on the pre-war Alvis, and with the 12/70's 4-cylinder engine it possessed adequate, if not sparkling performance.

The chassis of the Fourteen was wider and longer than that of the 12/70, but it retained the semi-elliptical springs and solid beam front suspension and leaf spring live rear axle. The body was also a straight take of the 11/70's and was a 'four light' design with traditional pre-war lines, a prominent grille flanked by a pair of large bar-mounted separate headlamps, sweeping but slightly bulbous front and rear wings, four doors and a bustle boot. The 12/70 engine was retained, but had its bore increased by 1mm to giving a bore and stroke of 74 × 110mm, with a capacity of 1892cc. The engine produced 65bhp at 4,000rpm, enough to give the car an acceptable performance.

Production of the bodyshell for the new car also posed a challenge. Originally it was intended to have Strachans of Acton produce the body, which was based on the 12/70

The TA14 chassis was based on that of the 12/70 and had beam front suspension. The fuel tank was hung on the rear end.

This view of the left-hand side of the 1892cc TA14 engine shows the single **SU** carburettor and its large air cleaner.

BELOW: **This 1948 TA14 was photographed at an Alvis Owner Club meet in the 1970s. The sombre lines and 'suicide hinged' front doors were typical of very early post-World War II cars and betray the car's 1930s ancestry.**

The TA14 came in saloon or drophead coupé bodies. This is a 1948 Tickford-bodied drophead coupé, which shows the hood fully down and room for four adult passengers.

saloon, with steel panels mounted on an ash frame. Strachans proved to be unable to get the bodies into production, so early in 1946 Alvis ordered Strachans to pass the tooling to Mulliners of Birmingham, who had made the 12/70 body in the 1930s. Again, production difficulties at Mulliners delayed the delivery of bodies to Alvis, where rolling chassis were being produced at the rate of some twenty per week.

The Mulliners body design was for a four-door saloon car with two windows on each side, that is, one in each door – a 'four-light' design. Alvis investigated other coachbuilders to produce bodies for the ever increasing numbers of bare chassis being produced and stored at its works, and commissioned Carbodies of Coventry and Tickford of Newport Pagnell to make drophead coupé bodies. The cheaper of the two drophead coupés was the Carbodies version, which was of welded construction, using pressed-steel panels. The Tickford version was a traditionally coach-built vehicle with extensive use of alloy panelling over ash frames and was the first post-war car body that the company produced. It was about one-third more expensive than the Carbodies product and an easy way to distinguish between the two versions was that the one made by Tickford had external 'pram irons' on each side of the rear section of the hood.

Both drophead coupé hoods had three positions – fully closed, partially opened with the roof above the front seat furled, or fully opened when the hood folded flush with the rear deck. Around thirty chassis were supplied to Duncan (see below) between 1947 and early 1948, and this company produced an attractive two-door pillar-less coupé body for the car. In addition to the Duncan, Alvis also supplied TA14 chassis, with wings, grille and bonnet, to a number of smaller coachbuilders. With the prevailing shortage of steel, many builders used wood to frame the bodyshell and alloy panels, and, due to the lower tax applied to working or commercial vehicles, many were built as estate cars or shooting brakes. Ultimately, though, the TA14 was produced in quantity in three main body types – a four-light saloon by Mulliners and the two drophead coupés by Carbodies and Tickford.

The TB14 – Sports Looks, if not Performance

The TB14 was an unusual departure for Alvis, as it was a two-seat sports car with a full-width body and surprisingly sporting looks. Based on a one-off special that had been equipped with a sports body built by F.J. Bidée, a Belgian

ALVIS *Individuality*

A striking combination of graceful line and quiet, effortless sports performance. This is a car outstanding for its *Individuality*—a thoroughbred in the true ALVIS tradition. Fully concealed one-man hood; ample luggage accommodation; furnished in high-grade leather, and beautifully appointed throughout.

THE FOURTEEN SPECIAL SPORTS TOURER

ABOVE: **The TB14 was a sports version of the TA with flowing bodywork. This is the prototype as shown at the September 1948 Earls Court Motor Show in London.**

Production TA14s had a more conventional front end with the headlamps in the wings. This is Adam Gilchrist's example, which he considers to be one of the best-looking cars ever made.

coachbuilder, the car had been commissioned by Belgian racing driver and industrialist Pierre Goldscmidt. In 1947, Goldscmidt entered it into the 2-litre class at 25 May 1947 Grand Prix de Frontières, which was held on a 6.75-mile (10.8 km) street circuit at Chimay in Belgium.

The car was displayed at the Brussels Motor show in February 1948, where it was called the 'Anglo-Belge' and Alvis took the idea on board, revamping the design into a road-legal two-seater with flowing lines. A prototype was displayed at the September 1948 Earls Court Motor Show and it generated a lot of interest from the public. The car featured a large chromed grille with the headlamps mounted behind it, a fold-flat windscreen, very large and substantial bumpers and wide styling strips running on the front wing to join with the side-lights mounted on them. With the body finished in red, and an ivory and red piped interior, the prototype's looks were praised. Even more attention was generated by the provision of a built-in 'Beauty Parlour' for the passenger, a cubby in the dashboard that contained tailored compartments for a mirror, lipstick and perfume, and a cocktail cabinet was built into one of the doors. The car was a two-seater and a lot of thought had been given to the hood.

The hood frame was hinged to the body and was designed to fold down into a space behind the seat back, which hinged forward to allow the hood to be stowed and concealed the hood completely when it was put back into place. This gave the car a very clean appearance with the hood down and was very convenient for the driver, with no loose hood irons and flapping fabric to contend with. However, problems arose getting the car into production – while the chassis was all TA14, finding a company to make the new body at a cost which kept the whole car's price below £1,000 to avoid double purchase tax proved difficult.

Eventually after a couple of false starts Alvis contracted with AP Metalcraft of Coventry to produce 100 bodies. By this time, the body design had been altered, with the head-lamps now conventionally mounted in the wings, the fripperies of the Beauty Parlour and cocktail cabinet deleted and the bonnet louvres dispensed with. The TB14 eventually started to be produced during 1950.

Production cars were fitted with a lightly tuned TA14 engine and twin SU H4 CV carburettors, which gave 68bhp at 4,000rpm, an increase of 3bhp from the standard unit. With a kerb weight of 2,772lb (1,257kg), which was some 364lb (165kg) less than the TA14 saloon, the TB had slightly better performance with a top speed of 80mph (129km/h) and

SPECIFICATION TABLE: 4-CYLINDER TA14

Engine

Type	Four-cylinder in line
Crankcase and block	Cast iron
Head	Cast iron
Cylinders	Four in line
Cooling	Water
Bore and stroke	74 x 110mm
Capacity	1892cc
Valves	Two per cylinder
Compression ratio	6.72:1
Carburettor	Single SU
Max power	65bhp

Transmission

Gearbox	Four-speed manual, all synchromesh
Clutch	Single plate

Suspension

Front	Solid beam, twin leaf springs
Rear	Live axle, leaf springs

Brakes

Type	Drums
Dimensions	
Track	54in (137.6cm)
Wheelbase	108in (274.3cm)
Weight (saloon body)	3,136lb (1,422kg)

Performance

Top speed	74mph (110km/h)

a 0–60mph acceleration of 19.9sec. However, this was not anywhere near the performance of the various new two-seat British sports cars that were starting to hit the market. For example, the 1949 Jaguar XK120 had a top speed of 124mph (200km/h) and 0–60 of 10sec, a performance that put the TB14 firmly in the shade. Eventually only 100 of the cars were made during 1949 and 1950, as competition from real sports cars like the Jaguar XK120 proved to be too much.

Only 100 TB21s were produced. The cars were fitted with twin **SU** carburettors and bodywork produced by **AP M**etalcraft of **Coventry**.

From the rear the TB14 shows its curvaceous lines and two-seat cabin.

The Duncan Coupé

One of the major issues that Alvis found with producing bespoke cars in the post-World War II era was the difficulty of procuring enough bodies to clothe the rolling chassis they were able to produce. One apparent solution to this appeared in 1947 when Duncan Industries, owned by aeronautical engineer Ian Duncan, produced a pillarless coupé body for Healey, which was also experiencing problems getting bodies produced. Duncan Industries was based in North Walsham in Norfolk and by chance Reliance Garage, an Alvis agent in Norwich, saw the prototype Healey and commissioned the design of a similar body for the TA14 chassis.

Under the pen of Frank Hamblin, Duncan's designer, a sleek two-door coupé body was designed for the TA14 chassis, which utilized the original radiator grille and bonnet, aligned with lightly revised front wings, rear hinged doors and sweeping lines. Not only was the body a much more modern looking affair than that of the TA14's defiantly pre-war looks, but it also featured pillar-less construction for the cabin, with the wind-down front and rear window disappearing into the bodywork to give a wide opening.

The Duncan's body was a traditional coachbuilding exercise, with an ash or beech hardwood frame clad in aluminium panels – thus avoiding the restrictions on the use of steel then in force. This was mounted on to the Alvis chassis and running gear. The only steel used in the body apart from the front wings and bonnet pressings were reinforcing sections in the door pillars and windscreen surround to reinforce the structure at the critical points.

As the body and its interior were designed around the Fourteen's chassis, it had just as much room as the saloon, although the rear headroom was not quite as generous and access to the rear seats was not quite as easy as on the saloon with its four doors. However, there was still enough space for four adults and it was luxuriously fitted out with leather seats and quality carpeting. Even the boot was a good size and the spare wheel was carried inside it. Thanks to the light alloy body panels, the dry weight of the Duncan Coupé was 2,912lb (1,321kg), which was some 280lb (127kg) lighter than the Fourteen saloon. This gave the car a bit of a performance boost to suit its sporting looks.

The main downside of the Duncan was its cost. Due to the expense of producing the new body, along with the swingeing rates of tax applied to all cars in the early post-war years, a Duncan Coupé cost nearly twice the price of the TA14 on which it was based. The Duncan factory went into receivership in 1948, with around thirty Alvis-based Duncan Coupés having been completed.

The Duncan Coupé body was produced by Duncan Industries of North Walsham in Norfolk, England. This shot shows the factory producing bodyshells, which were then mounted on to TA14 chassis.

Based on the TA14 chassis, the Duncan Coupé was an attractive and stylish take on the first post-World War II Alvis.

While it used the TA14 front wings and bonnet, the Duncan Coupé was all new from the scuttle back. Body panels were produced in lightweight aluminium sheet and ash or beech was used for the wooden frame.

TRICIA AND MIKE HARCOURT'S DUNCAN COUPÉ

Tricia and Mike Harcourt's 1947 Duncan Coupé was designed to be driven, and driven it is. The car has an extensive history, compiled by the previous owner, which revealed that the car's chassis was supplied to Duncan Industries on 12 April 1947, when it was fitted with body number 17, and as the car is fitted with a 'Brooklands of Bond Street' plaque, it is assumed it was supplied to the first owner by that firm.

Early ownership details are sparse, but the car was originally registered DFN 300, which was sold in 1987 and the car re-registered with the Northern Ireland plate FIL 5134. In 1973, the car resided in Tunbridge Wells and was red with silver wings and in a fairly poor state. The engine had been rebored and had a new crankshaft and big-end bearings to freshen it up. Without a doubt the next owner, Daniel Rowlands, saved the car when he bought it in 1973. He carried out an extensive programme of restoration work on the car during the 1970s, including the replacement of much of the ash body frame, which had succumbed after thirty plus years on the road.

Other work included re-tempering the rear springs, which had drooped, and lots of the chrome work was replated. New seat coverings in Vynide were fitted, along with a new headlining and carpets. Finally, after Rowlands

had had a bare metal respray done, he sold the car in the early 1980s. After another couple of owners, the car was resprayed in its current Dove Grey and it arrived in the Harcourt family in June 1999, having been bought by Tricia's father, Jim Tachell, who put the family's registration plate, JAT 39, on it. This was not his first Alvis – Tricia remembers that Jim had had an Alvis as the family car for many years and his idea of the ideal holiday was to go touring in an Alvis and covering 200 miles a day! Driving was his joy and even after he retired he continued to drive his Alvis cars as much as possible – to the extent of using a TA14 to visit every county in the UK in a year. Jim's last big trip in the car was to take it to the USA for the 2000 Alvis Owner Club USA Tour, taking along his grandson Timothy, who still enjoys driving the car (and the Harcourts' TA14 Mulliners Saloon) today. Tricia inherited the car from her father and has followed her father's example in driving the car.

The Harcourts find the car very practical for touring, as it is very airy and light inside, with comfortable seats (re-covered in leather to the original pattern by Jim in 2001) and while the car is not fast, it can still bowl along quite happily and cover the miles! Still in use and lovingly maintained by the Harcourt family, this Duncan Coupé looks to have a long and varied life ahead of it.

Tricia and Mike Harcourt's 1947 Duncan Coupé was owned by Tricia's father, Jim Tachell.

The Harcourts' Duncan Coupé is driven extensively by the family and is a familiar sight at Alvis Owner Club meetings.

The rear end of the Harcourts' Duncan Coupé shows the flowing lines that gave the Coupé a very modern and exotic look when it first came out in 1947.

The Duncan Coupé's interior is roomy in the front and with a wooden dash and a full set of instruments, it is a pleasant place to be.

CHAPTER EIGHT

POST-WAR
6-CYLINDER CARS

INTRODUCTION

After the end of World War II, the priority was to get a car into the showrooms both to keep the marque in the public's sight and to generate much needed revenue as wartime contracts were withdrawn. Alvis had planned to have a two-car range, with 4- and 6-cylinder models sharing the same chassis and running gear to maximize economies of scale and to ease production. With the TA14 in production, the company could look to the design and development of a new 6-cylinder engine to power the new addition to the range.

The New 6-Cylinder Engine

With the TC14's engine being designed in the mid-1930s it was really the final expression of pre-war engineering design, rather than a unit that exploited the latest thinking and could take advantage of the engineering innovations made during World War II. Virtually all of the other British manufacturers were in the same boat, but all were developing new engines that exploited the newly acquired knowledge and Alvis was no exception.

The first post-World War II Alvis 6-cylinder car was the Three Litre TA21. Produced from 1951, it had styling similar to the TA14, but had the headlamps faired into the front wings. This is the four-door saloon version with bodies by Mulliners.

THE THREE LITRE MODELS

Type	Description	Date
The Alvis-Healey	Alvis supplied engine for a Healey chassis and bodywork	1951–2
TA21	Four-door saloon bodywork by Mulliners, drophead coupé by Tickford	1951–5
TB21	Roadster bodywork based on that of the TB14	1951
TC21	Lightly updated TA21	1951–5
TC21/100	'Grey Lady', the first 100mph post-war saloon	1951–5
TC108G	Graber bodied for Europe; also by Willowbrooke for UK	1956–7
TD21	Graber style body built by Park Ward	1958–63
TE21	Graber style body built by Park Ward. First with twin stacked headlights	1964–5
TF21	Graber style body built by Park Ward	1966–7

The TA21 was also produced in drophead coupé form, where the body was produced by Tickfords.

Building on the knowledge gained producing its successful pre-war 6-cylinder engines, the first and only post-war Alvis engine that went into production was designed as a straight-6 ohv 3-litre unit. With a cast-iron one-piece crankcase and cylinder block, the new unit embraced the then current practice, marking a major change from the separate block and crankcase seen on the pre-war units. The treatment of the bottom of the engine was different to normal practice, as it was closed completely by a flat steel plate, which had holes cut into it for the oil pump and inlet strainer, and a cast-alloy sump was then bolted to the bottom of the plate. The cast-iron crankshaft was supported in the block on seven main bearings in line with the later pre-war unit's design, giving the crank the maximum level of support possible and making the overall assembly stronger at the cost of increased weight and friction losses. The crank was carried on Vandervell steel-backed thin shell white-metal main bearings, as were the big ends, ending the pre-war practice of having cast-in white-metal bearings that needed skilled hand working to ensure a precision fit and easing production effort. The connecting rods were steel 'H'-section stampings; gudgeon pins were clamped into the small ends and were free to float within the light alloy pistons. The pistons followed contemporary practice with three rings, the top two compression and the bottom one an oil scraper. The top compression ring was chrome plated to lessen cylinder wear.

The gear type oil pump was submerged in the sump towards the rear of the engine and picked up the oil via a floating gauze type filter. This was hinged on the oil pump to allow variations in the oil level. The gauze was the only oil filtration fitted and there was no external oil filter fitted to the engine, an oversight which was rectified later in the engine's life. Oil was fed under pressure to a gallery on the right-hand side of the engine, from which it was distributed through drillings to the main bearings, big-end bearings, camshaft bearings, timing chain and rocker shaft in the head. The oil from the rockers then drained down into the block, where it splash-lubricated the tappets and cam lobes and then made its way into the sump. Later engines were fitted with an external oil filter mounted on the right-hand side of the block and the oil filler was in the rocker cover. The oil was driven from the camshaft by a vertical skew gear, which also drove the distributor, mounted on the rear right of the block. The camshaft was mounted high in the right-hand side of the block in seven thin-wall white-metal bearings and was driven from the crankshaft by a duplex chain housed in a timing chest at the rear of the crankcase. It was tensioned by an automatic hydraulic pad type chain tensioner, which was pressurized from the engine oil.

The cast-iron cylinder head had polished kidney-shaped combustion chambers and the valves were positioned in line, allowing the use of a single straight rocker shaft. Tappet adjustment was made with a ball in the pushrod side of each

The post-World War II Alvis 6-cylinder engine was an all-new unit with modern monobloc construction, with the crankcases and cylinders incorporated in the same iron casting.

The new Alvis had twin **SU** carburettors as standard to help produce a decent power output.

rocker arm, which engaged with a cup in the top of the push-rod, was adjusted on a threaded shaft and locked in place with a nut. There was a light spring fitted around the top of each pushrod, which pressed against the head and kept the pushrod in contact with the rocker arm. This lifted the push-rod off the cam follower in the block. The intention was to take up any clearance at the top end of the engine when the engine was cold and to minimize noise from the top end – any noise made by the pushrod to cam follower was muffled by the crankcase. The inlet valves were made from silicon chrome steel and at 38mm in diameter these were larger in diameter than the 32mm exhaust valves, which were made from state of the art KE 965 austenitic stainless steel. The head bolts were positioned radially around each cylinder and a cast-alloy rocker box enclosed the top of the head.

The spark plugs were mounted slightly towards the exhaust valves to reduce pinking. The inlet and exhaust ports were colocated on the left-hand side of the block, with inlet ports 1 and 2, and 5 and 6 siamesed, and the centre two ports for cylinders 3 and 4 separate. In contrast exhaust ports 2 and 3 and 4 and 5 were siamesed, leaving ports 1 and 6 as single openings. The inlet manifold was fitted with a divider to separate port 1, 2 and 3 from ports 4, 5, and 6, and with a firing order of 1, 5, 3, 6, 2 and 4, the induction impulses were equally divided between the two halves of the manifold.

The cooling system was a conventional pressurized water system with an impeller water pump bolted to the front of

The engine was only given minor tweaks in the later 1950s when it was fitted to the Graber styled TD21.

the engine block, and a large capacity radiator and header tank. The water pump was driven from the crankshaft by the fan belt, which also drove the dynamo mounted on the right-hand side of the block. The fan was bolted to the front of the water pump drive pulley. Cooled water from the base of the radiator entered the block and flowed through a passage to the inlet side of the pump, where it was pushed up to the water passages in the cylinder head, with the passages designed to provide maximum flow around the exhaust valves and spark plugs. The heated water returned to the

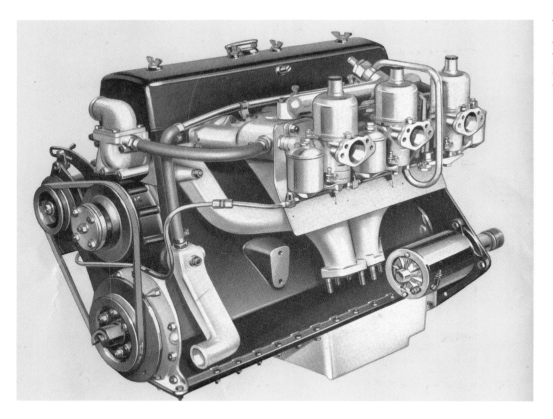

The final version of the Alvis 6-cylinder engine was fitted to the TF21 and had triple SU carbs to give a power boost.

top of the radiator via a thermostat mounted in an alloy casting bolted to the front of the cylinder head.

A mechanical fuel pump was situated on the right-hand side of the block and was driven from a camshaft lobe. It supplied fuel to the pair of SU constant velocity carburettors mounted on the inlet manifold on the left-hand side of the head. With a bore and stroke of 84 × 90mm, the engine was only slightly over-square, helping to limit piston speed and hence increasing reliability while still giving reasonable torque. With a capacity of 2992cc, the engine was justifiably called the Three Litre, and with a compression ratio of 6.9:1 (or 7:1 in some literature) it produced a claimed 90bhp at 34,000rpm and 150lb ft of torque at 2,000rpm. The engine was progressively developed through its lifetime and in its final form, fitted with triple SU carburettors, a new camshaft and a compression ratio of 9:1, the unit produced 150bhp at 4,750rpm.

While the new unit was not as advanced as the exceptional Jaguar XK and Lagonda straight-6 dohc cam engines, the Alvis engine was carefully designed for its intended market – an engine which produced adequate power, good torque and was quiet and reliable – perfect for the gentlemen's carriages that Alvis was producing.

The Alvis-Healey

One of the first applications for the new Alvis 6-cylinder engine was in a small two-seat sports car, the Alvis-Healey. The Alvis-Healey was a short-lived car based on the Nash-Healey sports car that Healey had designed for US manufacturer Nash, and which Healey produced in the UK for export to the US between 1950–4. The Nash-Healey used Healey's own design of ladder chassis and suspension design and had an all alloy body shaped by Italian stylist Pinin Farina that could be had in open-top or closed coupé style.

The Nash-Healey was fitted with a 4140cc Nash 'Ambassador Le Mans Dual Jetfire' engine, of straight-6 ohv design, and an automatic gearbox. The engine and gearbox had to be imported into the UK as bonded goods, which had to be returned to the US in completed cars to avoid Healey having to pay import tariffs. So while Healey had a pretty good design, to be competitive a UK version of the Nash-Healey would have to use a UK supplied engine and gearbox to avoid these import tariffs. So in the early 1950s, Alvis entered into a contract with the small-scale sports car builder to supply 250 of the new Alvis 6-cylinder TA 21 engines, where it was

ABOVE: **The Alvis-Healey was built in small numbers by Healey and was powered by the then new Alvis 6-cylinder engine. Based on the Nash-Healey sports car that Healey produced for the US market with a Nash straight-6, the Alvis-Healey was aimed at the domestic market.**

The Alvis-Healey has great looks and its styling obviously led to the mass-produced Austin Healey 100 with its cheap Austin engine. This example is owned by Adam Gilchrist.

The Alvis-Healey had a neatly trimmed interior, which unusually in sports cars of the time had wind-up windows. The traditional wooden dash had a full set of instruments.

From the rear, the Alvis-Healey's clean lines are apparent. The car was a practical and attractive bespoke sports car, but sales were limited by a high price.

used to power the 1952 Healey G-Type Sports Convertible, generally referred to as the Alvis-Healey.

This was an open-topped sports car that could seat two (or three at a squeeze) passengers side by side in the neatly trimmed cabin, and while based on the Nash-Healey it had a restyled all-aluminium body on a steel under frame, built by Panelcraft of Birmingham, in order to suit English tastes. It was fitted to a lightly revised Nash-Healey chassis and running gear designed to take the Alvis 6-cylinder engine. Healey's patented design of independent trailing link coil spring front suspension was used. This had a substantial cast-alloy trailing arm linked to a second casting, which held a coil spring and a lever arm damper that formed a top link. It provided a fair amount of wheel movement with no camber changes. At the rear, a live hypoid rear axle was fitted, which was located by two trailing radius arms on each side, with coil over-dampers providing springing and damping. A feature of the rear suspension was the length of the damper.

While the lower half was concentric to the coil spring, the upper half of the damper extended above the rear chassis rail and protruded into the boot of the car. The Alvis engine was lightly tuned over the TA21 unit, with a different camshaft, a slight increase to the compression ratio, up to 7:1

from the standard 6.9:1, and twin SU H4 carburettors, to give 106bhp at 4,200rpm. The Alvis-Healey was a neat and attractive roadster, with adequate performance, and benefited greatly from the flexibility of the Alvis engine giving it a top speed of around 100mph (160km/h) with the ability to pull cleanly from 10mph (16km/h) in top.

However, the car was somewhat weighty and very expensive and did not sell particularly well. Healey ended production of the Alvis-Healey after about twenty-five had been produced to concentrate on getting the Austin-powered Austin-Healy 100 into production. This was heavily biased towards using proprietary components from Austin to lower costs. Elements of the Austin-Healey styling, especially in the lines of the front lower section of the front wings, can be seen in the Alvis-Healey.

The TA21 Family

The new Three Litre Alvis, the TA21, appeared in 1951, and the model's styling was described by the *Autocar* magazine in 1952 as: '… what may be termed a modern version of traditional English coachwork'. To be honest, this was damning the car's

The TA21 entered production in 1951, but leant heavily on the TA14's pre-war styling. The four-door saloon could hardly be called innovative.

Looking very similar to the TA14 drophead-coupé, the TA21 version had the three-position hood and could seat four adults in comfort.

design with faint praise, while avoiding criticizing the model's obvious pre-war styling. The TA21 was available as a four-door saloon by Mulliners, or a drophead coupé by Tickford.

Styling wise, the TA21 saloon was not a great step forward from the TA14, retaining the earlier car's pre-war looks while the most notable departure from the TA14 body appearance was the fairing-in of the headlamps into the inner sides of the front wings. Otherwise, apart from being slightly larger, the TA21 was very similar in appearance to the TA14, with traditional flowing front and rear wings, vestigial running boards, side-opening bonnet and flat upright windscreen. The boot was longer and gave the car slightly more modern lines, as well as increasing the luggage space. Interior space was identical to the TA14. The new car was unveiled to the public in March 1950 at the Geneva Motor Show. A second car was taken to Geneva by John Parkes and was made available for test drives during the show, despite suffering from some problems with the cooling system.

The design of the bodyshell was improved over that of the TA14, with the intention of using less wood in the construction, in order to make the new car better suited to tropical climes. To that end, the central door pillar was made up from a light alloy casting and additional alloy castings were used in the rear wheel arches, adding strength while saving weight. As on the TA14, the doors were hinged on the centre pillar, making the front doors rear-hinged while the rear doors were front-hinged.

The TA21 chassis was based on that of the TA14, but with some significant differences, primarily the fitment of independent front suspension. The chassis was built up from two main longitudinal members made from closed 'Top Hat' sections, the rear part of which swooped up and over the rear axle. The front and rear of each longitudinal member had square section extensions, which were used to jack the car up using a 'Bevelift' jack. The extensions were accessed through the front and rear bumpers and were covered with rubber grommets with the Alvis logo embossed on them, a feature of all the TA to TF family of cars. The two longitudinal members were joined by six transverse cross members, four of which were closed square section and the remaining two of open 'U' section.

Apart from the 6-cylinder engine, the main differentiator from the TA14 was the independent front suspension. This was a double wishbone type, with the wishbones supporting a pivoting kingpin on which the hub was carried. Each wishbone was a one-piece type of welded construction, with the inners connected to the chassis with rubber bushes, while the outer swivels were of the threaded type. A coil spring and damper were fitted between the bottom wishbone and the chassis rail. The steering was designed to avoid any kickback and used two steering boxes – the main one positioned on the chassis longitudinally and operated from the steering wheel, which was connected to the secondary idler box on the other side of the car with a track rod. Two further track

This TC21-100 drophead-coupé is pictured alongside a 12/50 to emphasize the modern lines of the newer car. However, by the mid-1950s the style was looking dated.

Only produced in small numbers in 1951, the TB21 was a sports car based on the TA21, with its styling from the scuttle back taken from the TB14. Like the TB14, the bodywork was produced by AP Metalcraft.

rods took the movement from the steering box and the idler box to each front wheel, enabling these track rods to be the optimum length so that the wheel movement did not impart any unnecessary forces back into the steering.

At the rear, the live rear axle was suspended from semi-elliptical leaf springs and fitted with telescopic dampers. The brakes, drums front and rear, were 11in (279mm) in diameter and 2.25in (57mm) wide, were hydraulically operated and were twin leading-shoe operation all round. The TA21

drophead coupé was built by Tickford. Like the TA14 drophead-coupé, it was a two-door car with a three-position hood to provide open-top motoring in some comfort.

The TB21 Family

The TB21 was only produced in 1951 and was an attempt to replace the TB14 'sports' car. The TB21 shared its chassis and running gear with the TA21, including the 90bhp 6-cylinder engine. It also shared the TA21's body styling from the scuttle forward, keeping the imposing Alvis upright grille, side-opening bonnet panels and the headlamps faired-in to the insides of the front wings.

The styling from the windscreen back was similar to that of the TB14, with low-cut doors, a two-seater cockpit and a long, flowing rear end. With a bodyshell made by AP Metalcraft, the style proved unpopular with the public, although the 6-cylinder engine did improve the performance of the car over that of the TB14. The drophead coupé version of the TA21 provided the open-top motoring that the Alvis customer desired and the TB21 sold only thirty-one units during 1951, before being quietly dropped at the end of that year.

The TC21 Family and the Grey Lady

The TC21 was produced from 1953–5 and was a lightly updated version of the TA21. The bodywork was made by Mulliners, as with the TA21, and the main changes centred

around the engine, with the 6-cylinder's compression ratio raised to 8:1 and twin constant velocity SU carburettors fitted, giving a claimed 100bhp, up from the TA's 90bhp. This was made possible by the general availability of higher octane fuel across the UK. The second member of the TC21 family was the TC21/100, which was named the 'Grey Lady'. This was advertised as a true 100mph (160km/h) car, and differed from the standard TC21 is a number of minor ways. It was fitted with a higher 3.77:1 ratio rear axle (the standard TC21 had a 4.09:1 unit); the exhaust system was modified to improve breathing; the door pillars were slimmed down and the hinges concealed; the side windows gained chrome trim surrounds; and the top of the bonnet acquired a pair of air scoops, while 'Grey Lady' badges were positioned at the front sides of the bonnet.

Lucas 'Flarepath' fog and long-range driving lamps adorned the car's nose, one each side of the grille just below the headlamps, and chrome wire wheels on knock-on hubs completed the sporting looks. While the Grey Lady offered only a modest performance boost over the standard TC21, the car did have a top speed of over 100mph (160km/h) and gave

The first update to the TA21 was mainly mechanical and resulted in the almost identical TC21, first seen in 1953. This is the 100mph Grey Lady version, identifiable by the small air scoops on the bonnet.

The TC21-100 Grey Lady was lauded as the first 100mph saloon car available on the British market.

While it was a high-performance saloon, the Grey Lady's styling was still stuck in the 1940s. It was, however, a very good car.

Alvis a much needed boost in the marketplace, underlining and reinforcing the company's position as a supplier of high-quality sporting cars.

While the TC21 family, especially the Grey Lady, sold in reasonable numbers, Mulliners, which supplied the majority of the bodies produced, was always slow in producing enough bodies for the chassis produced by Alvis.

This supply issue came to a head in October 1954, when Mulliners entered into a formal agreement with Standard Triumph to supply bodies to that company exclusively, cutting off supplies of bodies to Alvis. The last TC21 was produced in 1955, and with Tickford having been bought by Aston Martin in that year, the car division at Alvis was staring closure in the face. The only hope for the future was the Swiss coachworks Graber, which had been clothing small numbers of Alvis chassis in modern and smart bodies since the end of World War II.

Modern Bodywork – Graber and the Last Alvis

Carosserie Hermann Graber of Berne was a Swiss coachbuilder with a long and illustrious history of building bespoke stylish cars for rich European customers. Formed in 1925 in the town of Wichtrach near Berne, the company specialized in producing appealing coupés and convertibles to very high standards of craftsmanship. During the 1920s and 1930s, the company produced bodies for chassis from manufacturers such as Alfa Romeo, Bugatti, Panhard, Bentley and Duisenberg.

The post-war period saw Graber forge close relations with the British car industry and the company became the Swiss distributor for Alvis in 1955, cementing a relationship that started in 1945 when Graber first began producing one-off bodies for the Alvis TA14 chassis.

By the early 1950s, Graber's main body design for the Alvis TC21 chassis had evolved into a handsome and modern looking two-door four-seat coupé or convertible with full-width bodywork, restrained and attractive lines that made the TC21 look dated and staid. However, possibly fortunately for Alvis sales, Graber's cars were mainly sold in mainland Europe, with swingeing import tariffs preventing their sale in the UK. Even in Europe, the cars were expensive, though they sold in small but reasonable numbers. With most of the Western European countries emerging from the dust of

World War II into a period of economic growth, increasing prosperity and a gradual return to normality, the market for expensive and exclusive bespoke cars was picking up, albeit in a much larger market than the UK alone, and Graber's relatively small operation, building limited numbers of bespoke cars, was well suited to address the emerging markets.

Alvis and its dealer network were aware of the Graber models and did seriously look at the possibilities of importing Graber-bodied cars in the early 1950s, but the cost of the Swiss bodywork and the prospects of the impending Issigonis TA175 and TA350 projects mitigated against the possibility of selling the Graber cars in the UK. Things changed rapidly in 1955, with the cancellation of the Issigonis project and the removal of Mulliners and Tickford from the open market. This left Alvis with the ability to make its rolling chassis, but with no way to build the bodywork to clothe the chassis. In 1955, Alvis commissioned Graber to build two coupés, based on a pair of right-hand drive TC21/100 rolling chassis, which were supplied to Graber during 1955. Graber worked quickly and the cars were displayed at the Paris Motor Show in October 1955, the London Car Show at Earls Court, also in October, as well as the Scottish Moor Show held in November. After being displayed, both cars were registered in the UK as SHP642 and TDU810 and at the time of writing were both still in existence.

It took Swiss coachworks Graber to show Alvis the way ahead. Built on a TC21-100 chassis, this is an early Graber TC-108G drophead coupé with its modern full-width bodywork and a style that would carry Alvis into the 1960s.

The first attempt to produce a Graber style body in the UK resulted in the Willowbrook cars. Unfortunately, Willowbrook proved to be unable to meet the order and only fifteen or sixteen Willowbrook-bodied TC106/G cars were produced.

After the Willowbrook problems, Alvis turned to established coachbuilder Park Ward to produce its cars. This is Jonathan Huggett's 1961 TD21 drophead coupé.

**The TD21 'saloon' was a two-door coupé and this is Martin Slatford's
1962 TD21 Series II.**

The cars were well received at home and abroad and orders started to flow in. In the meantime, Alvis had been exploring the possibilities of licensing the design for production in the UK and searching for a coachbuilder who could take on the work. Graber was happy to license the design and the firm of Willowbrook, based in Leicestershire, was chosen to produce the bodies. The new Graber body was described by Alvis as: '... one of the most beautifully proportioned cars ever offered to the British public. The exterior is matched by an equally attractive interior, faultlessly trimmed and luxuriously appointed.'

Graber's masterpiece was introduced in 1956, with the new full-width coupé body based on the TC 21/100 Grey Lady chassis, which at a stroke rendered the TC21 Three Litre's existing and old-fashioned 1930s styling obsolete.

One of the two Graber produced prototypes, SHP642, was road-tested by the *Autocar* magazine in March 1957, where it received a pretty good report, with only the rear seat leg and headroom, the instrument panel switch layout and the brakes' ultimate performance being criticized.

The car's performance, handling, suspension, steering and interior trim were all singled out for particular praise – when a magazine describes the ride as being as 'smooth as a seagull riding a leisurely breeze', you know the writer must have been impressed! The conclusion was that the car was very good and if the customer had the money 'it is hard to think of a better way of spending it' than to buy an Alvis. The Graber body style gave Alvis a timeless design that would remain in production for the rest of the 1950s and into the 1960s.

JONATHAN HUGGETT'S TD21 DROPHEAD COUPÉ

Jonathan Huggett is the TD registrar of the Alvis Owner Club, and, as one would expect, he owns an immaculate 1961 TD21 fitted with a drophead coupé body by Park Ward. Painted in Alice Blue, the car is an older restoration and Jonathan bought it from a contact in Canada, reimporting it back to the UK in 2013. His prime reason for buying it was to give him something to drive while his TC100 Grey Lady was being restored, and since then he has used the TD21 extensively. Fitted with the 3-litre 6-cylinder engine and an Austin BN7 four-speed manual gearbox, the car also benefits from having an overdrive fitted by Jonathan to help with long-distance cruising.

Another job Jonathan did was to replace the sagging rear springs with slightly stiffer TF units. Apart from these jobs, the car has been pretty reliable, needing little more than routine servicing and the fitment of an auxiliary electric fuel pump to overcome a fuel vaporization issue. As a long-distance cruiser, the TD is excellent and bowls along happily at motorway speeds, although it is a little tardy at getting going initially. It is a comfortable and relaxed car to drive, and with the roof down the wind noise is surprisingly low and the cabin relatively draught-free. It is fitted with modern Vredestein Sprint Classic tyres, a brand popular with classic owners, which run true and have good wet grip, although they do make the steering heavy at low speed. Jonathan values the car's ability to cruise far and fast and one of his best trips in the car was returning home from an Alvis South West meeting in Taunton in 2017, when everything came together to give a great drive on the rolling English roads back to his home just south of London.

Jonathan Huggett's 1961 Three Litre TD21 Series I drophead coupé is an early Park Ward car. The subject of a very good restoration in Canada, the car gets lot of use.

With the neat Graber styling and Alvis name, the TD21 is the epitome of 1960s style.

From the rear, Jonathan's TD 21 drophead coupé is an attractive grand tourer.

The Willowbrook Cars – TC 108/G

Production of the new Graber style bodyshell was still an issue for Alvis. With Mulliners and Tickford out of the picture and most of the other true coachbuilders either closing down or swallowed up by the major car makers, options for producing the new body were limited. While Graber could have produced them, the cost of an imported body with the import tariffs added rendered that approach uneconomic. With its options limited, Alvis went to Willowbrock, which as first glance seems a strange choice. Willowbrook, based in Loughborough in Leicestershire, was a well-established company that concentrated on literally building coachwork – bodies for coaches and double-decker buses. What it did have was the experience of producing bespoke hand-crafted bodywork on traditional chassis. However, the company was not experienced in producing high-end bespoke motor cars, or costing their build.

The main elements of the bodyshell, including the front and rear wings, the bulkhead, inner panels and front and rear panels, were made from 18-gauge sheet steel, and the bodyshell was assembled and welded together off the chassis on a jig before being fitted to the chassis. The car's roof, bonnet and boot lid were aluminium, while the floor, which was fitted directly to the chassis, was made of marine ply. Graber had supplied jigs for the main elements of the body, but these were wooden formers designed for low-volume production.

The main problem with building the new body was that all the panels had to be hand-formed. The Graber design incorporated a number of elements that gave the body rigidity and, when firmly mounted on the chassis, gave the whole car a much more rigid structure. At the front, the radiator grille surround incorporated a tubular steel hoop which was rigidly fixed to the chassis to stiffen up the body and the front cross member, while a pair of steel members ran forward from the top of the scuttle to the bottom of the radiator hoop.

These measures were combined with a scuttle structure that was designed to be very stiff. With carefully designed front wheel boxes and welded-on front wings, the whole

The Willowbrook cars were very similar to the later Park Ward cars, but had wood floors, lower rear boot lines and different rear lights. This car was converted to left-hand drive when exported to Canada, but has since returned to UK shores.

The traditional Alvis grille was an important styling feature of the Willowbrook cars and defined the front end. The frontal appearance changed very little when production was taken up by Park Ward.

front end of the car very strong. The main body sills were substantial box sections that were bolted to the chassis side rails and four points on each side, and the box section was continued to form the base of the scuttle structure. Like the front, the rear wings were welded in place, making the rear end strong as well. The only weak spot on the body, which has come to light after many years' service, was the 'A' post uprights, which were made of wood, but were not substantial enough and have been found to be prone to wear where the hinges attach, allowing the doors to sag.

While the Willowbrook cars were based closely on the original Graber produced cars, they were improved in some areas. The rear seat squab was repositioned to give a bit more leg and headroom for the rear seat passengers. The control layout was improved – the cars were fitted with a glass-fibre dash panel, with the main instruments positioned in front of the driver, and the steering column was adjustable. The wrap-around rear screen was produced in three sections, with a neat slim chrome bar running from the roof to the rear deck on each side to seal the join between the main central screen and the side elements.

With a contract to produce the new bodyshell for Alvis, Willowbrook struggled both to make the bodies in the time calculated and to meet the original costings – the bodies proved to be much more labour intensive to make than Willowbrook originally thought, so production was very slow and costs were high. Production of the bodies started in May 1956, but by October only three had been completed. The lack of cars led to rumours that Alvis was getting out of the car business, causing potential customers to think twice about ordering a car, especially as Alvis was unable to give an accurate delivery date. By the end of 1957, only fifteen or sixteen Willowbrook cars had been completed and orders were dropping off as customer interest was waning.

In the meantime, Graber, which was still producing its version of the car for the Continental market and had recently introduced a soft-top version, was complaining that it could not get enough rolling chassis from Alvis to meet its order book, as chassis production had been slowed to avoid unused chassis backing up at the factory.

The Willowbrook cars had a neatly integrated instrument panel. Made from glass-fibre, it positioned the dials in front of the driver.

The rear seating in the Willowbrook was plush and comfortable, but headroom in the rear was limited. This was rectified in the Park Ward cars by lowering the seat squab and raising the roof slightly.

Park Ward's ability to produce car bodies in some numbers saved Alvis car production. This TE21 from the mid-1960s was pictured at an Alvis Owner Club meet at a damp Newlands Corner in Surrey.

The Park Ward-Bodied Cars – TD21, TE21 and TF21

With the production problems at Willowbrook causing major delays to the delivery of cars, something had to be done. Alvis contacted Boulton and Paul, the wartime aircraft manufacturer, and Jensen to provide estimates for the production of the bodyshell, but these did not lead to any firm commitments. Eventually, Alvis was to go to one of few remaining traditional coachbuilders, Park Ward of Willesden, London. Park Ward had been set up by William McDonald Park and Charles W. Ward in 1919. By the early 1920s, they were producing bodies for Rolls-Royce, which bought a minority stake in Park Ward in 1933 and in 1936 unveiled a new 'all-steel' body for Rolls-Royce and Bent-

ley chassis. In 1939, Rolls-Royce bought out the remaining capital in the company and Park Ward became a fully owned subsidiary of Rolls-Royce. Post-World War II, Park Ward was used to produce bespoke bodies for Rolls-Royce, along with Rolls-Royces from the other London-based coach-builder, Mulliners.

In 1961, Rolls-Royce merged Park Ward with Mulliners, a company well known to Alvis as it produced the Alvis TA21 and TC21 saloon bodies. As bespoke work for its parent company was tailing off, Mulliners Park Ward was in a position to take on work for Alvis to keep the Willesden works busy. The manufacturing technology and methods available at Mulliners Park Ward meant that the company was able to give a competitive quote for the production of bodies for Alvis, mainly through the use of a rubber stretch press to

The TD21 was an attractive car with lines that were fully up to date in the 1960s.

The interior of the TD21 was a feast of leather and wood. The instrument panel on the Park Ward cars moved back to the centre of the dash in a backward step from the Willowbrook cars.

form the main steel body panels, rather than beating the panel to shape by hand. The rubber-based tooling was significantly cheaper to produce than the steel bucks used to mass-produce panels, and while the tooling was not as accurate or as long-lasting as a steel buck, it was suited to the relatively small numbers of bodies that were produced.

Panels produced on the tooling still needed to be hand-finished, but the labour involved was much less than that required to hand-form the panels from scratch over a wooden buck, as Willowbrook had been doing. A second change was the use of flat steel sheet to form the floor of the bodyshell, rather than Willowbrook's plywood. The steel floor sheets were spot-welded into place on the body, which added to the stiffness of the bodywork. These more efficient methods of manufacture meant that the bodies

were cheaper to produce and Alvis was able to introduce the new car at a significantly lower price than that of the Willowbrook models.

The shift to the new body supplier also enabled Alvis to make a number of changes to the Willowbrook specification. The nose acquired on each side of the radiator two horizontal rounded rectangular air-intake vents that were fitted with wire protective grilles with a chrome surround, as well as a plain central triangle that mimicked the Alvis badge, but had no lettering on it. The left-hand intake fed fresh air to the heater, a larger 3.5kW unit based on the system fitted to contemporary Bentleys, and the one on the right-hand side fed air to the AC air filter fitted to the twin SU carburettors.

Under each of the 7in diameter headlights were a pair of round lights – an amber indicator above a smaller white side

The rear seats of the **Park Ward** cars were still plush and comfortable and had more headroom than the **Willowbrook** cars.

With the hood down, the Graber styled Alvis was an elegant and refined tourer. This is a 1964 TE.

MARTIN SLATFORD'S ALVIS THREE LITRE SERIES II TD21

A couple of years ago, Martin Slatford was looking for a classic, with some particular requirements. He wanted to use it for classic rallies, so it had to have the ability to cover long distances, be comfortable, be a good motorway cruiser, be reliable and be in good enough condition to be presentable, but not in such good condition that he would be afraid to use it. Finally it had to be a reasonable price, well made, English, have good spares availability and be practical. The result was his rather nice 1962 Alvis TD21 Series II.

The car is virtually standard, with only a retro-looking modern DAB radio and a neatly integrated satellite navigation set to disturb the time-warp interior. Martin likes the Alvis – he finds it to be a very competent grand tourer with enough performance to keep up with today's traffic – the 130bhp engine and five-speed ZF box helps here – and he loves the period vibe that the car exudes. The only downside is the lack of power steering. At speed the steering is fine, but it gets to be quite hard work at when parking. Martin finds it instructive to compare it with his early 1970s Rover P6 3500 – a similar driving experience, but with lighter power steering, and lacking the 1960s period charm of the Alvis.

Martin has used it on a rally to Spain, to help to raise money for charity and the only real problem that Martin has experienced arose on that rally. The water pump bearing bolts holding the fan and pulley on to the water pump spindle sheared and the petrol pump diaphragm failed, causing fuel starvation especially when going up hills. This resulted in the car getting a lift home on a trailer. Other than this easily sorted issue, the car has been reliable, usable and a joy to own.

Martin Slatford stands by his 1962 Alvis Three Litre TD21 Series II. The dark grey paintwork complements the Graber styling nicely.

Martin's TD21 was bought so that he could drive it on national and international classic rallies. The recessed spotlights on the front panel were only featured on the Series II.

The TD21 has performed well in Martin's hands and he is very pleased with it. It looks lovely and performs well, is comfortable and reliable and is well suited to its role as a grand tourer.

From the rear, the Park Ward cars were neat and cleanly styled. The drophead coupé had a large rear window, giving good visibility.

From the front, the clean lines of the TD are apparent. The spotlights were mounted on the front bumper in the Series I TD as seen here on Jonathan Huggett's example.

Here is a close-up of the front end of Martin Slatford's TD Series II, showing the recessed driving and fog lights. Air was drawn into the heater and carburettors around the lights.

marker. On later Series I cars, the side markers grew to be the same diameter as the indicators. The changes combined to give a significant update to the frontal appearance of the car, and were complemented by a pair of secondary lamps, driving and fog, mounted directly on circular plinths fitted on to the front bumper. The space for the rear seat passengers was increased by lowering the floor level – helped by the adoption of the steel floor panels – which increased the headroom, and by repositioning the pedal box forward, so that the driver's seat could be moved forward, again giving more legroom to the passenger behind. The instrument panel went back to the traditional wooden type, with the instruments positioned in the centre of the dash to suit both left- and right-hand drive applications.

At the rear of the car the top wing line was raised and the boot was enlarged so that it could carry two sets of golf clubs, while the rear window became one piece with slightly less wrap-around than the three-part type seen on the Willowbrook. New rear lights were fitted and the number plate was fixed on the rear panel with its associated light.

Alongside the sports saloon, Alvis also produced the elegant drophead coupé version. While sharing the exterior dimensions and lower body style of the saloon, the drophead coupé had a fully upholstered and lined hood, which, when lowered, dropped back almost completely into a well around and behind the rear seat, where it could be covered with a clip-on cloth tonneau. This detail ensured that the car avoided the 'folded pram hood' appearance of many contemporaries.

The main styling change between the TD and the TE was the adoption of twin
'stacked' headlights on the TE, as shown in the 1964 TE21 Series III.

The TE21's stacked headlamps, rectangular rounded air intakes each side of the grille and bumper-mounted spot- and fog lights are all typical of the later Park Ward cars.

The TF interior saw the dash updated, with the instruments relocated into a binnacle in front of the driver in line with the then current ergonomic practice. It gave the car's interior a more up to date feel.

The last Alvis car to be built was this **Three Litre TF21 Series IV**, now in the possession of Adam Gilchrist. The exterior is virtually identical to the **TE21**, with an updated interior and lightly revised mechanical components justifying the new designation.

SPECIFICATION TABLE: 6-CYLINDER POST-WORLD WAR II ROAD CAR – TA21 TO TF21

	TA21 1951	TF21 1967
Engine		
Type	Straight six	Straight six
Crankcase and block	One piece cast iron	One piece cast iron
Head	Cast iron	Cast iron
Cylinders	Six in line	Six in line
Cooling	Water	Water
Bore and stroke	84 x 90mm	84 x 90mm
Capacity	2993cc	2993cc
Valves	Two per cylinder	Two per cylinder
Compression ratio	7:1	9:1
Carburettor	30mm Solex	Triple SU
Max power	90bhp	150bhp
Transmission		
Gearbox	Four speed all synchro	Five speed ZF
Clutch	Single plate	Single plate
Suspension		
Front	Independent, coil spring and wishbone	Independent, coil spring and wishbone
Rear	Live axle, semi-elliptical leaf springs	Live axle, semi-elliptical leaf springs
Brakes		
Type	11in (28cm) diameter drums, twin leading shoe, front and rear	Front: 11.5in (29.2cm) disc Rear: 11in (28cm) disc
Dimensions		
Track	54.5in (138cm)	54.5in (138cm)
Wheelbase	121.5in (308.6cm)	121.5in (308.6cm)
Weight	3,472lb (1,578kg)	3,360lb (1,524kg)
Performance		
Top speed	89mph (143km/h)	120mph193km/h)

ADAM AND CLARE GILCHRIST'S ALVIS COLLECTION

With a thriving top-end bespoke carpet business that keeps Adam Gilchrist and his wife Clare busy 24/7, it came as a surprise to find that they had a lifelong addiction to Alvis and possessed a selection of post-war cars to delight even the most fastidious collector.

With his interest in the marque sparked by his father, a successful lawyer, Adam and Clare have collected many examples of the Graber styled cars, including a unique left hand drive Willowbrook-bodied TC108G and the last car Alvis made, a TF21.

Along with a lovely TB14, which Adam rates as one of the best-looking cars ever, and a very rare Alvis-Healey sports car, bought by Adam for Clare after she fell in love with it at an Alvis International meeting, the selection of coupé and drophead TC, TD and TFs covers virtually every Graber style model made. All the cars are kept in great working condition. These are not garage queens, taken out in covered trailers for display at rarified Concours d'Elegance events, but are working, driving active vehicles kept in fine mechanical and cosmetic condition that do much to raise the public's awareness of the Alvis marque.

A frequent visitor to Alvis events, Adam and Clare relish driving the cars and all their children are also insured to drive the cars – inducing the next generation into the delights of Alvis ownership. So why Alvis? Adam's mother was confined to a wheelchair and the acquisition of his father's first car, an Alvis TF, meant that his family could travel together – previously all travel had to be by train when the family would be consigned to the guard's van as there was little or no provision made for wheelchairs.

So the Alvis represents freedom to Adam as it so radically changed the family dynamic, making it possible to travel on their own terms. Adam finds when driving the cars in his collection that problems seem distant and happy childhood memories come to the fore – as he puts it, they are a wonderful TARDIS transporting him back to those happy days of youth. Adam's father's TF is currently nearing the end of a long restoration under his brother Luke's custodianship and once it is on the road it will be a lasting testament to Adam's parents and the happy childhood they gave him.   And this is what classic cars are all about. It's not just the nuts and bolts, paint and bodywork, smells and noise, it is the memories of loved ones, good times, places and events that the cars evoke, kept alive by long-term ownership. And that's what Adam and Clare get from their collection – it reminds them of the past and the cars are still being used to generate ever more enjoyable memories for them and their children.

Adam and Clare Gilchrist have an impressive collection of Alvis cars. Shown here are (from left the right) their Alvis-Healey, 1965 TE21 convertible, 1964 TE21 saloon, 1964 TE21 convertible and TF21 saloon.

Adam poses with his 1965 TE21 convertible.

This is how Adam likes his Alvis cars – roof down on a sunny day, all ready for a nice long drive.

Adam's Alvis-Healey is a rare car with a racing history.

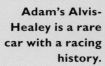

The last Alvis made poses alongside the TF convertible with the Surrey hills forming the backdrop.

Each of the Graber-built cars was different, being designed to customer requirements. This 1957 TC108/G shows Graber's own design of grille, but it is still recognizable as a late Alvis.

The last of the Grabers were very stylish. They had a significantly lower body line and looked very sleek and exotic. This Graber Super Convertible was pictured at the British Motor Museum.

The Alvis solution gave the car an elegant, smooth appearance when the hood was down; the only disadvantage to this solution was a slightly narrower rear seat. The hood mechanism was manually operated and was a complex mixture of steel hoops and wooden formers, which enabled the relatively large hood to fold into the confined storage space behind the seats. When up, the hood's robust construction and lining were waterproof and kept out the noise, making the convertible a practical year-round grand tourer. One early customer for the TD21 was HRH the Duke of Edinburgh, who drove a drophead TD21 during the 1960s.

The first of the cars to be built by Park Ward was the Alvis Three Litre TD21, which was introduced in late 1958 for the 1959 model year and was available in saloon or convertible form. At last, Alvis had a body supplier which could produce a good quality product at an affordable price and in enough quantity to satisfy demand, while the Willowbrook-bodied cars trickled on to the market in tiny numbers. Around 784 TD21 Series Is were built between 1959 and December 1961. The main mechanical change from the TC21 was the option of Dunlop disc brakes to replace the front drums.

The Alvis Three Litre Series II TD21 heralded a return to a complicated naming regime by Alvis. The car was introduced in January 1962 and was a minor refresh of the TD21, which was retrospectively referred to as the Alvis Three Litre TD21 Series I.

The main external change was that the two front fog and driving lamps were repositioned in recesses in the front panel, replacing the Series I's two small grilles and giving a more integrated look to the front of the car. About 285 TD21 Series IIs were built Between January 1962 and mid-1963.

The next model to appear in 1963 was the Alvis Three Litre Series III TE21 – it is unclear as to why TD was changed to TE, but the main distinguishing feature was the adoption of two 5.75in (146mm) diameter headlights fitted one on top of each other on each front wing, giving a virtually unique appearance. The main mechanical change to the Series II was the fitting of Dunlop disc brakes all round, with 11½in (292mm) diameter rotors on the front and 11in (279.4mm) diameter rotors on the rear.

The twin spotlights in the front panel of the TD models were deleted. The engine was tuned to give 130bhp at 5,000rpm by increasing the diameter of the inlet and exhaust valves by 2mm, enlarging the inlet and exhaust valve ports to take advantage of the larger valves and using a larger

diameter tubular tuned exhaust manifold. The TE21 had the option of ZF power steering from 1964 and the fitting of a five-speed S5-17 type ZF gearbox or a BorgWarner three-speed automatic. About 349 TE21 Series IIIs were built between mid-1963 and March 1966.

The final model to appear, in March 1966, was the Alvis Three Litre Series IV TF21. Virtually identical in appearance to the TD21, the car was fitted with a new ZF five-speed manual box, the S-520, as standard, with the option of a BorgWarner three-speed auto box. Mechanical changes included a significant engine tune, with triple SU carburettors fitted to a water-heated manifold, which, along with a rise in the compression ratio to 9:1 and larger valves, pushed the engine's output up to a healthy 150bhp.

At the rear, variable rate springs were fitted to the rear suspension to improve the ride and tighten up the handling, while the handbrake acquired a self-adjusting mechanism. The interior of the TF21 also came in for some updating. Its instruments moved from the centre of the dash into a cowl in front of the driver, giving a boost to the ergonomics – and reverting back to the overall layout (if not the same design) seen on the Willowbrook-bodied cars. A larger heater was fitted and the rear window was electrically heated. Produced until 1967, the TF21 was the last car manufactured by Alvis and approximately 105 were built.

Graber's Own Interpretations

All the time that Willowbrook and then Park Ward were making bodies for Alvis, Graber was pressing on making its own unique bodies on chassis supplied by Alvis. While the first cars tended to be similar to the UK-produced design, the radiator grilles often received different treatment, moving from the traditional upright design with a chrome surround to a more contemporary look, often incorporating an 'egg-box' style inner grille. As Graber was in the business of making bespoke cars, the design element evolved with each car the company made and no two were the same – while sharing the overall design, the details would be tweaked on each car so as to make them unique.

The ultimate Three Litre Alvis was the Graber Super Alvis. Produced in both saloon and cabriolet versions, the Super featured a bodyshell that was significantly lower than the 'normal' Graber styled Alvis. This gave the car a much sleeker and more up to date look than the Park Ward cars.

With its stacked headlights, the Graber gives a nod to the Alvis coupé, but the wide and low grille emphasizes the Graber's wide and low looks.

The Graber Super Convertible's interior is luxuriously appointed with a very neat instrument binnacle and retains the Alvis-badged steering wheel boss.

With a low rear deck and neat styling touches, the **Graber Super** is attractive from all angles.

The Graber Super was also produced as a coupé. This example was pictured in Red Triangle's showrooms in 2018.

The last Alvis, the Three Litre TF21 Series IV, was pictured by Alvis under this ancient archway.

Aside from the lower overall style, the front gained a wide and low oval grille with a small Alvis badge in its centre and a wide air scoop dominated the top of the bonnet. The car echoed the lines of the classic 1960s GT cars from Aston Martin, Ferrari and Maserati and was a fitting finale to the Alvis line.

Alvis sold the last three TF chassis to Graber, which were delivered between October 1967 and February 1968, and were clothed in Graber Super Alvis style bodies.

CHAPTER NINE

POST-WAR MILITARY VEHICLES

INTRODUCTION

After World War II, the experience Alvis possessed in small AFVs and cross-country load carriers was at last recognized and the company was awarded a contract in 1947 to design and develop a family of six-wheel drive vehicles with good (if not outstanding) cross-country performance. The contract resulted in the development of four distinct vehicles: an armoured car and personnel carrier (FV601 and FV603); an unarmoured prime mover (the FV620 range); and an airfield fire tender (FV652). The contract awarded to Alvis for the various vehicles in the range kept the factory busy with both home and export orders through to the 1970s.

The second range of fighting vehicles produced under the Alvis banner was the Combat Vehicle, Reconnaissance (Tracked) abbreviated to CVR(T), which was designed to replace the various FV601 and FV603 armoured vehicles and to fulfil other tasks. Designated the FV100 family, two unique features of the range of vehicles was the use of aluminium alloy to build the hull, making significant weight savings over a steel hull, and a militarized Jaguar XK 4.2-litre engine producing 195bhp, which gave the lightweight vehicle outstanding performance. The range was introduced to British Army service in the late 1960s and early 1970s, and the Scimitar, Spartan, Samaritan, Sultan and Sampson were still in service in 2018 when this book was written, a lasting testament to the skills Alvis demonstrated in designing the range.

The first post-World War II military vehicle Alvis produced was the six-wheeled FV600 family. Shown here are (left to right) the Saladin armoured car, the Saracen Armoured personnel carrier and the Stalwart amphibious prime mover. Missing is the Salamander fire tender.

The second family of military vehicles Alvis thatproduced post-World War II was the FV100 series of tracked armoured vehicles. Left is the Scorpion with its 75mm gun and to the right is a Scimitar with a 30mm cannon.

THE SALADIN, SARACEN, SALAMANDER AND STALWART

The first vehicle in the range was the FV601 Saladin, which was a heavy armoured car designed to replace the British Army's current World War II vintage armoured cars, the Daimler Mark 2 and AEC Mark III, both four-wheeled vehicles. With a newly designed 76mm gun as its main armament housed in a power-operated turret, the Saladin was a formidable upgrade in capability and with its six wheels, all-independent suspension and powerful rear-mounted Rolls-Royce 8-cylinder engine, it offered good performance both on and off road. The Saladin's development was delayed by the need to get the Saracen into service; the Saladin went into service in the late 1950s.

The FV603 Saracen was the second member of the family of vehicles. While retaining the FV601's overall layout, with Rolls-Royce 8-cylinder engine and six driven wheels, the Saracen had the engine mounted in the front and a large armoured box-type body with room for eight troops who entered and exited through a pair of rear doors. A machine gun was mounted on a small turret for protection. Prototypes were prepared and presented to the Ministry in mid-1950 and a production contract given for 150 vehicles in October 1950. The haste was due to the need to get the vehicle into production to support operations in Malaya, where an insurgency had broken out. Both the Saladin's and

Saracen's hulls were sealed to enable them to cope with water obstacles of up to 3½ft (1,070mm) without any prior preparation.

The third and fourth members of the FV600 family were unarmoured, but were still six-wheel drive vehicles with an excellent cross-country ability and decent performance, They shared the Saladin's rear-engined layout. The FV651 and FV652 Salamanders were fast cross-country fire tenders. These were needed by the RAF as it entered the jet age and deployed faster and heavier aircraft, which required a corresponding upgrade in the capability of the RAF's fire fighters.

The FV620 Stalwart was an amphibious cargo carrier designed to deliver supplies to units situated close to the front line without relying on roads or bridges in the European theatre of the Cold War. With the Soviet forces poised for a blitzkrieg style assault across the central plains of Europe, planners needed a flexible response to absorb the first thrust and ensure that a counterattack could be mounted. To this end, logistics were as important as front-line forces, as a tank force without fuel or ammunition was useless. While the military was looking at the tracked FV432 Armoured Personnel Carrier (APC) family as a possible source as a cargo carrier, the cross-country credentials of the FV600 vehicles had been amply demonstrated by the Saladin and Saracen, and Alvis was confident that it could produce a vehicle that would meet the requirements. The

The Saladin was a heavy armoured car. Its six wheels gave it good mobility and the 76mm gun had the hitting power of a World War II medium tank.

The Saracen armoured personnel carrier could carry up to nine troops in its rear passenger compartment as well as three crew members. The Saracen was the only member of the FV600 series vehicles to have a front-mounted engine.

The last of the line was the Stalwart, designed as an unarmoured amphibious load carrier with the mobility to support main battle tanks in the field.

result was the FV622 Stalwart, a unique vehicle that could carry around 5½ton (5,588kg) of cargo, could swim and had unmatched cross-country performance.

As an aside, the FV600 design competition also included an armoured car from Straussler based on the Hungarian 'Hunor' design. Like the successful Alvis design, it was also a six-wheel drive, as was a second submission, the Straussler 12ton, Amphibious Armoured Car or AAC/12 (DD Type), both of which were unsuccessful.

THE FV600 FAMILY POWER TRAIN – ENGINE, GEARBOX AND FINAL DRIVE

All of the Alvis six-wheeled range shared similar engines, gearboxes and drive trains, although the various configurations were tailored to each vehicle's layout. One aspect of the design was that the vehicles were not powered by an Alvis engine, but by a Rolls-Royce unit that was designed to be the standard British Army power plant for small to medium vehicles. The reasons for this were clear and the result of forward thinking by the military planners. During World War II, the British Army had used a myriad vehicles that were produced by a range of domestic manufac-

turers, along with Commonwealth and US manufacturers. This meant that there was a lack of standardization across the range, with lots of different components in use, such as engines, transmissions and running gear, which gave rise to problems supporting the vehicles in service.

The problem extended down to the basic engineering standards used – for example, most British vehicles used a range of thread forms for their nuts and bolts including British Standard Fine (BSF), British Standard Coarse (BSC), Whitworth and even British Standard Pipe (BSP), while the majority of US vehicles used the Society of Automotive Engineers Unified threads (in both fine UNF and coarse UNF pitches) and Canadian goods could use either, or in the worst case both!

While all these threads worked well, they were incompatible and required workshops and field engineers to carry extra tools and spares. While unavoidable during the war, post-war policy was to design common elements where possible that would conform to the then current standards. This became even more important with the formation in 1949 of the North Atlantic Treaty Organisation (NATO), which was created as a military alliance of the Western nations to oppose Russia and the spread of Communism. One of NATO's core objectives was to ensure interoperability among the Allied armed forces by establishing defined engineering standards.

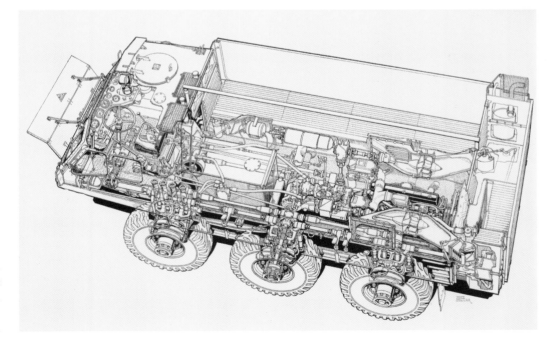

This cutaway diagram of the Stalwart shows the basic chassis layout of the FV600 family, as well as the suspension and drive components.

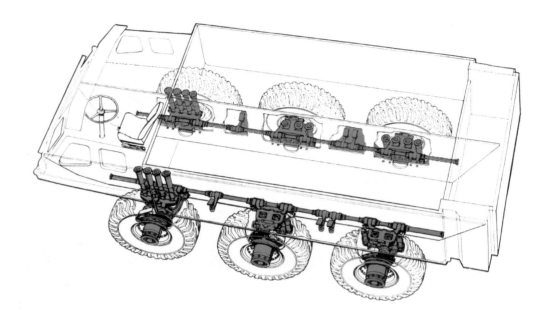

Each of the six wheels of the FV600 chassis was independently suspended on wishbones and was sprung using longitudinally mounted torsion bars.

One of the fruits of this drive for standardization was the development by Rolls-Royce of a family of petrol engines for use in British Army vehicles – the B-Series Engine (not to be confused with the British Motor Corporation's B Series, as used in many Morris, Austin and MG cars of the 1950s, 1960s and 1970s). The Rolls-Royce engine was initially based on a standardized bore of 3.5in (88.9mm) stroke of 4.5in (114.3mm) and originally came in three formats: the B40 was a straight 4-cylinder with a capacity of 2.8 litres, the B60 was a straight 6-cylinder with a capacity of 4.25 litres and the B80 was a straight 8-cylinder with a capacity of 5.675 litres. A further development, the B81, was a 6.5-litre unit with a revised 3¾in (95.5mm) bore, giving a capacity of 6522cc.

All the engines in the range burned petrol in line with the then current British Army's policy to have all its vehicles from cars to tanks running on a single type of fuel. The design was inlet over exhaust, with the inlet valves in the cylinder head and the exhaust valves in the cast-iron block. With this valve configuration and 2 valves per cylinder, the engines were not powerful, with the first Saladin's B80 engine producing 160bhp at 3,750rpm, but produced outstanding levels of torque at 257ft lb at 1,750rpm, giving the right power characteristics for the military applications for which the engines were designed. The standard bore and stroke meant that the engine range used common parts for most of the moving (and hence wearing) parts – pistons, connecting rods, piston rings, valves, valve springs and so

on. They also had common main and big-end bearings, all of which meant fewer line items needed in the stores. All of the Alvis six-wheel drive vehicles were powered by various versions of the 8-cylinder B80 Rolls-Royce engine.

The first production B Series engines were made with British Standard threads, but production shifted to all Unified threads during the 1950s. In the case of the Alvis vehicle, this meant that the first 250 Saracens were fitted with the BS threaded Mark 3A B80, which also had an alloy cylinder head, while subsequent Saracens had the Unified threaded B80 Mark 6A engine, which was also fitted to the Saladin. The Salamanders and Stalwarts were fitted with the larger and more powerful B81 6522cc unit.

In the Alvis vehicles, the transmission was broadly based on that seen on the Daimler Dingo scout car, but adapted to allow for the extra two driven wheels. The engine drove a five-speed gearbox. The gearbox drove a transfer box, which was mounted on the rear of the gearbox. This transfer box had two functions – to give forward and reverse functions and to distribute the drive to all six wheels. This was achieved by having a system of six bevel boxes, three on each side of the hull, and each box driving a single wheel. The two central bevel boxes were positioned one on each side of the transfer box; each had one input shaft and three output shafts, two oriented fore and aft and one facing outwards. The two fore and aft shafts took drive to the front and rear bevel box

Seen here is the upper and lower wishbones, above which are mounted the dampers. The thick running fore and aft torsion bar operates on the inner end of the top wishbone. The curved steering arm is apparent.

This cutaway shows the main features of the Saladin armoured car and the crew positions.

on that side of the hull. Each of the six bevel boxes had an articulated driveshaft fitted with a pair of Tracta universal joints to transmit power to the wheel. The wheel hubs themselves contained a set of planetary gears that reduced the overall gearing. On the vehicles, the hubs and transmission joints in the hull were waterproofed to allow for wading, but also swimming in the case of the Stalwart and the 'Floating' Saladin.

The suspension was fully independent using double unequal length cast-steel wishbones on each wheel. Four shock absorbers were fitted to the rear four wheels, two for damping and two to control rebound, while the front wheels only had three dampers, with only a single rebound damper to give adequate clearance for the steering mechanism. Springing was by longitudinal torsion bars, operating on the top wishbones. The steering system was a power-assisted hydraulic recirculating ball type, which operated on the front and central wheels. The centre wheel linkage geometry was designed to give less movement to the centre wheels so as to preserve the correct geometry. The wheels fitted to the FV600 family were standard War Department split rims, made from aluminium alloy and 20in in diameter and were bolted on to the hubs.

FV601 SALADIN ARMOURED CAR

The initial contract awarded to Alvis for the development of a wheeled AFV came about from a concept originally developed at the Fighting Vehicles Research and Development Establishment (FVRDE) at Chertsey for a replacement for the then current medium-weight armoured cars, the four-wheeled Daimler Mark II and the AEC Mark III. The Daimler was developed from the Dingo scout car, but was larger and carried a 2-pounder (40mm) gun and coaxial 7.92mm Besa machine gun mounted in a turret. It was of monocoque construction, with the 16mm thick welded armoured hull forming the chassis and body. It had the 95hp 6-cylinder Daimler four-stroke engine sited at the rear and all four wheels were driven. It had independent coil spring suspension all round and a five-speed preselector gearbox with transfer box. It weighed in at 7.5ton (7,620kg). The Daimler was mainly used for reconnaissance in support of infantry and tanks.

The AEC Mark III was another four-wheeled armoured car and used a large number of components from the AEC Matador tractor. Powered by a 7580cc diesel engine, the first diesel engine used in a British UK armoured car, the

A preserved Saladin at the Aldershot Military Museum. Note the sloping front armour and the short-barrelled 76mm gun.

transmission was part-time four-wheel drive with the front wheels normally driven and a transfer box to engage the rear wheels when required. In the Mark III the turret mounted a 75mm gun and a coaxial 7.92mm Besa machine gun. The vehicle was considerably heavier than the Daimler at 12.7ton (1,290kg), mainly due to the use of 30mm armour plate. This heavy armour and powerful gun meant that the AEC was assigned to the heavy troops of armoured car regiments to support the lighter armoured cars in the other troops.

In order to replace these two armoured cars, the requirement was set by FVRDE for a relatively heavy vehicle, originally with a crew of four, that would be capable of engaging and defeating light and medium tanks, while remaining significantly lighter and more agile and, although wheeled, retaining a cross-country performance that was close to that of a tracked vehicle. Hence the FV601 Saracen had to balance the three requirements for all tanks – agility, armament and weight – to provide good cross-country performance, a powerful gun and as little weight as possible. The specification called for a multirole vehicle, covering reconnaissance, the pursuit and harassment of retreating enemy armour, and the engagement with enemy infantry, soft-skinned vehicles and enemy armoured cars. The end result

was a specification for a six-wheeled, all-wheel drive vehicle, with an armoured steel monocoque hull and a 76mm gun mounted in a power-operated turret and weighing around 10ton (10,160kg). The vehicle was rear-engined, perpetuating the 'standard' armoured car layout first seen in the 1930s Alvis Straussler AC30.

Alvis was given a development contract for the vehicle in October 1947, but the programme was delayed, as the Saracen APC was given priority. With its development programme restarting when Saracen development was completed, the Saladin eventually went into production in 1956, when an order for 169 vehicles for the British Army was awarded and deliveries commenced during 1959.

FV601 Saladin Design and Development

Development of the Saladin started with the award of a development contract to Alvis in 1947 to develop the FVRDE's specification for a new armoured car for the British Army into a workable entity. The specification that defined the overall layout of the proposed vehicle had already been produced, so Alvis's job was to refine the outline design into

From the rear, the Saladin shows its engine cooling slats on the rear deck and the rather slab-sided turret.

a workable vehicle and produce a production-ready design, along with all the associated drawings. These could then be put out to industry to tender for the production contract.

While the specification had been broadly fixed, the original crew was envisaged to comprise four men. The proposed armament was the World War II vintage 2-pounder gun (37mm) gun and there was a second rear-facing steering position, again just like the 1930s Alvis Straussler AC3. However, the 2-pounder was not considered to be powerful enough to defeat equivalent vehicles, even with a device called 'Littlejohn' fitted, a sleeve which let the gun fire a smaller calibre round with a higher muzzle velocity and hence the penetrative power of the armoured piercing shell. The gun was also incapable of firing high-explosive rounds, another important requirement. Unfortunately, there was no existing gun that was small enough to fit in the proposed turret. There was a new 76mm gun under development that would be ideal, although it would not be ready until the early 1950s.

By April 1948, Alvis had produced a wooden mock-up and by September 1949 it had produced a full-sized prototype, FV601A, albeit without the turret, the design of which could not be finalized until the gun design was complete. By the end of 1949 it was apparent that there would not

be a contract for the Saladin production in the immediate future, as the urgent need for the Saracen APC was becoming apparent.

Development of the Saladin had to take a back seat as Alvis ramped up production of the Saracen and the design of the new 76mm gun was finalized. One major change from the original specification was forced on the project by the new gun – it took up more space than the original 2-pounder, so the crew requirement was reduced to three, with the commander also aiming and firing the main gun. This resulted in the crew roles being commander/gunner, loader and driver and also led to the deletion of the second rear-facing steering position. Development continued and in 1953 Alvis produced a second prototype, FV601B, which was broadly speaking to a production standard.

FV601 Saladin Description

The Saladin had an all-welded armoured steel hull, which housed the crew, engine transmission and turret. The hull was divided into three compartments: the front housed the driver; the middle below the turret ring was the fighting

This picture of the Saladin shows the vehicle deployed in foreign climes. Note the open driver's hatch and the coaxial machine gun on the turret mantlet.

compartment; and behind the turret was the engine compartment. The driver's compartment held all the controls and seating for the driver, and had two means of entry or exit – a top hatch sited on the front of the turret ring, while access could also be made from the fighting compartment when the turret was suitably positioned. The driver could see out through the open front hatch and when closed down used three periscopes for vision, one facing forward and one on each side.

The all-welded armoured steel turret was designed for a two-man crew, housing the commander/gunner and loader. It rotated on a turret ring made up of ball bearings in a track, which was situated on the top of the hull. The turret extended downward into the fighting compartment to form a turntable and the two crew members' positions were fitted in this turntable, with the gunner on the left and the commander on the right, so the turret crew positions were fixed relative to the turret. Cut-outs in the turret extension allowed access to the driving compartment and various ancillary equipment mounted in the rear of the fighting compartment, which included the batteries, carbon-dioxide cylinders for the engine compartment fire-suppression system and the drinking water tank. There was also access to the two escape hatches fitted each side of the hull just below the turret ring.

Eleven rounds of 76mm ammunition was stored in the turret turntable between the driver and the gunner, a fur-

ther twenty-three rounds were stored in the driver's compartment and eight were stowed in the rear left-hand side of the hull outside of the turret turntable. The 76mm gun and 50-calibre coaxial machine gun were mounted on a glacis plate to allow up and down movement of the guns. The gunner had a dual periscope with a 6× magnification element for sighting the gun and a 1× magnification for observation. The commander had four observation periscopes arranged around the front edge of his hatch and a swivelling periscope to give him rear vision.

The radios were fitted into the rear bustle of the turret. The turret had a power-assisted turning mechanism, which was backed up with a manual winder should the assisted mechanism fail. On top of the turret were two access hatches and a mount for an anti-aircraft machine gun. There was a pair of storage bins fitted on each side on the top of the outer hull sides.

One unusual feature that was only fitted to the Saladin was its brakes. FVRDE had designed the brake in the late 1940s, when there were concerns that the weight of the Saladin would overwhelm the drum brakes of the time. The revised brakes were a composite drum/disc design known as a ring brake and were produced to the FVRDE design by Borg & Beck Lockheed. They had a friction-lined centre plate attached to the inside of a conventional drum. The centre plate was acted on by an inner pressure plate, which,

The steeply sloping front armour is apparent in this shot of the front quarter of the Saladin.

The Saladin was a useful addition to the British Army's equipment, replacing Its World War II vintage heavy armoured cars. It was produced from 1952, with the last example delivered in 1972, and was sold worldwide.

when it was hydraulically activated, moved outwards from the hub and pushed against the inside edge of the centre plate. This action also bought an outer pressure plate into contact with the outer edge of the centre plate as the drum floated between the two plates.

The Saladin was not developed into other roles like the Saracen and there was only one version, the Mark 2 (Mark 1 was assigned to the prototypes). However, there was a variant of the Mark 2, the 'Floating' Saladin, which was designed to capitalize on the Saladin's existing wading ability and offer an amphibious capability. The 'Floating' Saladin was a standard Saladin fitted with a lightly modi-

fied superstructure, which enabled the fitting of a canvas 'camera bellows'-style waterproof screen, similar to those used on World War II tanks. The screen ran round the perimeter of the hull, above the wheels, and was sealed to the hull. The screen was raised by a pair of manually operated winches and a clear plastic insert was fitted so that the driver could see where he was going. Propulsion and steering while floating were provided for simply by the movement of the wheels and no special propulsion units such as those on the Stalwart were fitted. The screen and its associated fitting added some 495lb (225kg) to the overall weight of the vehicle.

In 1966, Alvis started to build two prototype 'Stalwartized' Saladins, which were powered by the Stalwart's larger and more powerful Rolls-Royce B81 Mark 8B engine. With a capacity of 6516cc, it produced 220bhp at 4,000rpm and 312lb ft of torque at 2,400rpm, a considerable increase over the Mark 2 Saladin's 160bhp B81 Mark 6D. The new engine needed the gearbox and cooling system to be uprated and only one of the prototypes was completed, but apparently it drove very well with a much enhanced performance. However, the concept was not taken any further.

FV601 Saladin Production

Saladin production started in 1952 and continued until 1972, when around 1,650 had been produced. The British Army only took some 243 vehicles, with the rest of the production going to a wide range of export customers, including Australia, Ghana, Hong Kong, Indonesia, Iraq, Jordan, Kenya, Kuwait, Lebanon, Libya, Nigeria, North Yemen, Oman, Portugal, Sharjah in the UAE, South Africa, Sudan and Uganda.

Some also went to the West German border police, the Bundesgrenzschutz. The majority of these West German Saladins were sold on to Honduras. During the late 1960s and early 1970s, Australia mounted Saladin turrets on the US M113 A1 APC to create a fire-support vehicle. In 1990, during Iraq's invasion of Kuwait, television film emerged of Kuwaiti Saladins being used to oppose the invaders in Kuwait City. In 2016, Indonesia commissioned local defence contractor Pindad to update the country's Saladins so as to keep them in service for several more years.

FV603 SARACEN ARMOURED PERSONNEL CARRIER

The Saracen APC was specified to replace the US-supplied half-tracks that the British Army had used in World War II to carry troops into battle across country and to provide a reasonable degree of protection from small arms fire. The contract to develop Saladin was awarded to Alvis at the same time as the Saracen armoured car contract and the

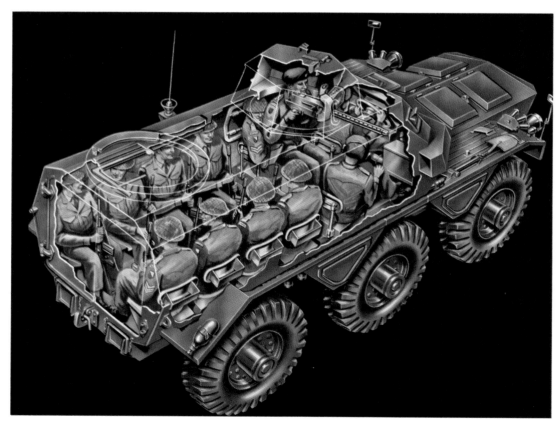

The Saracen APC's interior layout is seen in this cutaway. It was a tight fit for nine armed troops along with the commander, driver and gunner.

intention was for the two vehicles to share a significant number of components while using different hulls. However, the Communist-led insurrection in Malaya that started in June 1948 meant that the requirement for the Saracen APC was deemed more urgent than the Saladin, so Alvis switched most of its resources to developing the Saracen and getting it into production as soon as possible. Initially in the Malayan Emergency priority was given to protecting the populated areas, then moving into the countryside to seek and destroy the insurgents in fights chosen by the British. This meant that there was a requirement to move troops safely around the country, escorting convoys and patrolling the contested countryside, and the nascent FV603 was considered ideal to meet this need.

FV603 Saracen Design and Development

The Saracen was designed to carry twelve people – three crew (driver, commander and machine-gun operator) and nine passengers. With the deployment in Malaya in mind, the overall width of the vehicle was constrained to be under 8ft (2,438mm), as this was the spacing between trees used in the rubber plantations across Malaya, which the vehicle was expected to patrol. The second constraint was the require-

ment to have the passenger compartment long enough to carry a standard stretcher, anticipating the use of the vehicle in the armoured ambulance role. With the engine and running gear based on that used in the Saladin, there was one problem – the Saladin was rear-engined and the Saracen needed to fit the engine in the front to allow for the crew and passenger compartment. However, this was relatively easy to overcome, as the transfer box allowed for forward or reverse running in all five gears, although the steering mechanism had to be repositioned.

With the basic layout of the vehicle defined by the FVRDE specification, Alvis's role was to productionize the vehicle, produce prototypes and get the vehicle into production as quickly as possible. The first prototype was built and tested by Alvis in early 1951 and was delivered to the FVRDE in June 1951, where acceptance tests were carried out. Two further pre-production vehicles were rushed out to Malaya for field testing in early 1952. The tropical conditions and relatively harsh environment uncovered problems with the hydraulic accumulators used to store the pressure of the hydraulic system that powered the brakes and steering. In addition, the cross-country performance was limited by the lack of a differential lock, which meant that if all the wheels on one side lost traction, for example if they were on a soft verge while the other side was on a road, all the power would be

As the only front-engined version of the family, the Saracen's troops embarked and disembarked through the rear door, or through a hatch on the roof behind the turret.

diverted to the spinning wheels, stranding the vehicle. Heat soak from the engine compartment also raised the temperature of the floor at the front of the vehicle to unacceptably high levels.

FV603 Saracen Description

The Saracen's hull was made from armoured steel plate and had two compartments. The engine was in the front compartment, with the higher crew compartment taking up the rest of the hull. The engine compartment had a louvred front to protect the radiator from bullets and the top of the engine compartment had four (two each side) hinged access panels. At the front of the crew compartment was the central driving position and the driver had a central front-facing hatch that was used for access and, when open, gave the driver a good view ahead. When closed, the driver had to use a periscope incorporated in the hatch for forward vision. Behind the hatch, the hull side sloped back at around 45 degrees to join the outer sides of the main passenger compartment and a further two hatches were positioned, one on each side, which afforded a side view to the driver. As with the front hatch, these side hatches were fitted with periscopes for when the hatches were closed.

Immediately behind the driver's seat was the commander's seat, which was height adjustable to give access to the small roof-mounted machine-gun turret. To the right was the third crew seat. On the front left was one passenger seat and running down each side of the compartment were four more passenger seats, facing inwards. Three small arms ports with hinged armoured covers were fitted on each side of the compartment. Ventilation for the occupants was provided by four electric fans, two each side, which had mushroom-headed covers mounted on the upper side of the hull. The rear door was a two-part side-hinged design with a pair of small arms ports fitted, one on each leaf. On top of the hull of the APC variants was a small turret for self-defence. This carried a .30 calibre machine gun, with a 360-degree manual transverse, and there was a sliding hatch over the rear of the passenger compartment that had a mount for a .303 Bren gun for use in the anti-aircraft role.

The suspension followed the Saladin's lead, with twin wishbones supporting each wheel and torsion-bar springing, and the brakes were conventional drums. Between each pair of wheels was a triangular storage box, which also acted as a mudguard.

One problem that arose with the Saracen was keeping the occupants cool when it was deployed to desert regions. When heat soak from the engine and transmission was combined with high ambient temperatures, the interior temperature rose rapidly, with detrimental effects on the occupants. The solution was to reverse the flow of cooling air through the engine bay, pulling in air from the rear of the engine compartment and pushing it out forward through

Pictured at the Aldershot Military Museum, this Saracen shows how the front-mounted engine needed armoured grilles in the front to let cooling air into the radiators while providing protection from small arms fire.

The reverse-flow cooling system meant revised air intakes on the front of the Saracen. The revised cooling system helped to keep the cabin cool when the Saracen was used in hot desert environments.

This front view of the Saracen shows its slatted armoured radiator intake, driver's viewing hatch in its closed-down position and the turret with its machine gun.

the radiator. This was achieved by replacing the rear engine access lids in the rear of the front deck with louvred towers nicknamed 'beehives' to allow air into the rear of the engine compartment, the fit of Saladin engine fans to direct the air forward through the radiator and fitment of a new front panel that blanked off the existing air intake in front of the radiator and directed the airflow up and over the bonnet. The louvres in the beehives were fitted with armoured baffles to prevent small arms fire entering the engine compartment. Vehicles so fitted were designated FV603C.

There were two more modified Saracens that warranted their own 'FV' numbers: an Armoured Command Vehicle (ACV), designated FV604 and FV610(a), and an armoured ambulance designated FV611. The FV604 ACV was essentially a lightly modified FV603 with a reconfigured interior including a comprehensive command radio fitted with stations for three or four radio operators, an exterior generator to power the radios and the ability to fit a canvas tent around the back of the vehicle to give more (unarmoured) space. There were additional steel plates welded to the top of the passenger compartment to provide locations for the tent. The FV610(a) APV was a later and more comprehensive development of the Saracen ACV and was built to a specification produced by the Royal Artillery. Essentially it was similar in specification to the FV604, but had an extensively modified passenger compartment with raised hull sides that gave a lot more interior armoured space for the radio operators.

The ambulance version, FV611, was based on the hull of the FV603, with an interior fitted out to carry three stretchers on its left-hand side and two seated patients, or a total of ten seated patients. A crew of two comprised a driver and a medical orderly.

FV603 Saracen Production

The Saracen was rushed into production and the first examples were shipped to Malaya for testing in early 1952. Delivery of production vehicles started in May 1952

and by September of that year production was running at around twenty vehicles a month. As well as being of great use to the British Army, Saracen was an export success for Alvis, with sales to overseas customers starting in the late 1950s. Customers included Bahrain, Indonesia, Jordan, Kuwait, Libya, Nigeria, Qatar, Sharjah in the UAE, Sri Lanka, Sudan and Thailand. The Saracen remained in service with the British Army and RAF in decreasing numbers and in various roles until as late the early 1990s, by which time it had been largely replaced by a combination of the larger tracked FV432 and the smaller CVR(T) FV103 Spartan.

FV651 AND FV652 SALAMANDER FIRE TENDER

The FV651 and FV652 Salamanders were fast cross-country fire tenders, which were contracted for in 1954. The need such vehicles was as a result of the ever increasing weight, performance and size of RAF aircraft as the service embraced the jet age. Research had shown that the best chance of saving survivors of an aircraft crash was to get the crash site in under three minutes and smother the wreckage with foam to extinguish any fire before it took hold. The existing fire tenders in service did not have the performance in terms of speed, cross-country ability, or the capacity to carry sufficient volumes of fire suppressant to deal with major crashes, so the Ministry of Supply (MoS), along with the War Office, drafted a specification for a high-performance fire tender.

The Salamander chassis was essentially that of the Saladin, with a rear-mounted engine and six-wheel drive.

The Salamander's Pyrene-built body incorporated a 'Monitor' foam gun above the cabin and hoses mounted on the side of the body. The rear-hinged doors enabled the crew to exit quickly at a crash site.

The Salamander with its six-wheel drive was capable of rapid response to aircraft crashes on the large airfields of the RAF. The Salamander was in service with the RAF from the mid-1950s.

With its excellent cross-country ability and proven chassis and mechanicals, a vehicle based on the FV601 and FV620 was an obvious choice. With its potential for military and civil aviation applications, the design process was owned by the MoS.

FV651 and FV652 Salamander Design and Development

Salamander development commenced during 1953, when a series of trials were held at the FVRDE and the Alvis factory, represented by the front-engined Saracen, was deemed the most suitable. While tracked competitors displayed better cross-country ability, the Saracen chassis combination of higher road speeds, lack of damage to runways and good-cross country ability, along with the potential for the carriage of a significant payload when rebodied without the weight of the armour plate meant that it was the favoured participant, and Alvis was granted a development contract from the MoS in 1954. The contract gave the new vehicle an initial designation FV6001 and named the vehicle 'Salamander', a creature that the Ancient Greeks thought could live in a fire.

The major change from the Saracen used in the trials was the adoption of the rear-engined Saladin chassis to form the basis of the new vehicle. Alvis retained the Saladin's layout and mechanical parts and fitted them into an unarmoured all-steel plate chassis with the driver right at the front with a high seat position. The need for a good performance meant the fitting of a larger capacity engine, the 6522cc Rolls-Royce B81 Mk8, The chassis was fitted with a new body design by Pyrene, based in Brentford, West London, which also fitted out the new vehicle with its fire-fighting equipment.

The prototype displayed some issues, which included steering 'chatter', a lack of performance and poorly set-up suspension. Pyrene's cab was criticized for a lack of grab handles for the crew, which meant that they were flung about when the vehicle manoeuvred at speed, and the forward hinged doors hampered fast exits from the cab. Alvis constructed a second prototype chassis with fixes for the problems. It was fitted with a Rolls-Royce B81 Mk 8B engine that had been tweaked by Rolls-Royce to give a healthy 235bhp at 4,000rpm, revised power steering valving and revised suspension settings, while the Pyrene produced cab had grab handles and rear hinged doors. In January 1956, the MoS granted a production contract for forty chassis units, which were delivered by the end of 1958 and around this time the vehicle designation was changed to FV651.

FV651 and FV652 Salamander Description

The first production version of the FV651 Salamander was given the designation Truck, Fire Crash, Foam Mark 6 by its main customer, the RAF, as the previous airfield fire truck was the Thornycroft 5ton 6 × 6, designated the Mark 5. Based on the chassis of the rear-engined Saladin, the Salamander chassis was constructed of welded mild steel plate and followed the lines of the FV601 unit. The chassis had additional box-section side units and cross members added to it to replace the torsional rigidity lost with the removal of the Saladin's upper hull elements. The Rolls-Royce B81 Mark 8B engine was positioned at the rear of the chassis with its radiator mounted behind it and the transmission followed the layout of the Saladin. The front steering position was positioned centrally and the driver's seat was further forward and higher than the Saladin's to give the drive a good view and to allow the crew of six easy access to the two rear-hinged doors for rapid egress at a fire scene.

The body carried a fire-fighting system that was powered from the Power Take Off (PTO) mounted on the engine. The system was capable of producing 9,000gal (40,900ltr) of foam, which was pumped on to the fire using either a 'Monitor' foam gun mounted on the top of the cab, which could deliver all the foam on to a crash site in two minutes, or from a pair of 60ft (18,290mm) hoses. A further 16gal (73ltr) tank containing chlorobromomethane, a clear colourless liquid used to smother fires, was also fitted. This liquid was delivered via a pair of 100ft (30,480mm) long hose units.

The FV652 was a Canadian Air Force model, which had an enhanced capability to shoot foam from the Monitor on to a crash while still driving. This led to a modification to the Canadian vehicles' Power Take Off to enable it to operate the Monitor mechanism while the vehicle was in motion. The second tranche of orders for the UK was based on the FV652 chassis and were designated FV652 Mark 6A.

FV6651 and FV652 Salamander Production

The production of Salamanders was relatively small, with a total of around 125 units being ordered and delivered during the 1950s. There was only a relatively small export market for the vehicle, with the Royal Canadian Air Force taking thirty-four and the Royal Ceylon Air Force taking one.

One aside from the Salamander was the one-off adoption of a Salamander as a 'Runway Surface Testing Vehicle'. Designed for the Ministry of Aviation and the Road Research Laboratory (based near Bracknell, Berkshire) in the early 1960s, a Salamander had its centre two wheels removed and was converted to four-wheel drive. A test wheel, which could be fitted with an aircraft tyre plus the associated lifting and braking mechanism, was installed in the centre of the chassis between the front and rear axles, along with measuring equipment. A load of up to 5ton (5,080kg) could be imposed on the central wheel and the whole piece of kit was used to measure the coefficient of friction between the tyre and various runway surfaces under test.

FV620, FV622 AND FV62 STALWART HIGH MOBILITY LOAD CARRIER

The final member of the FV600 series of vehicles was the FV620 Stalwart. The vehicle was designated the High Mobility Load Carrier (HMLC) and was designed to support the Cold War scenario of NATO forces operating to counter a Soviet invasion of Western Europe. This scenario was based on the destruction of the road infrastructure and fast-moving armoured fighting formations needing rapid resupply anywhere in the battlefield, which could potentially stretch across the whole of Western Europe. It was assumed that there would be no time in which to replace blown bridges or repair roads, so the HMLC would need to have a cross-country performance close to, if not equivalent to, a tank, as well as a true amphibious capability that would enable the vehicle to swim across rivers where no bridges existed.

The Stalwart was the fourth of the FV600 family. A high-mobility load carrier, it was designed to transport ammunition and supplies to forces in the field.

The current inventory had nothing suitable – the Army's existing trucks had limited cross-country performance and had no amphibious capability, so would be unable to keep up with a formation of tanks. A new vehicle was needed and initially the War Office was looking at using the new FV432 tracked APC, which was being trialled as a basis for the new requirement. However, Alvis was able to point out the advantages of a wheeled vehicle over a tracked one in the role, as wheeled vehicles would be faster, quieter, easier to maintain, more fuel efficient and cheaper to make than the FV432 derivative.

In 1957, Alvis was given a contract to produce a prototype HMLC, which would be based on the Salamander hull. The result was the Stalwart, a 6×6 truck with a forward-control cab and a large but high loading bay. The running gear was taken from the Salamander and as it was broadly the same as that used in the Saladin and Saracen, it was easily capable of carrying the required cargo of around 5ton (5,080kg).

Stalwart Design and Development

Alvis started the design and development of the Stalwart as a private venture in 1957 and by the end of 1959 a prototype, designated PV1, was up and running and undergoing testing by Alvis. It was based on a Salamander chassis, with a long, flat load platform with drop-down sides. The cab was a shortened Salamander, as the vehicle only required a two-man crew. One downside of PV1 was that the use of a standard Salamander chassis meant that the load bay had a large hump in it to accommodate the engine air inlet and radiator cowling, and tests showed that this was not at all practical. PV1 even floated with a bit of temporary waterproofing, but had no dedicated water-propulsion system, relying on the driven wheels and steering to navigate while afloat. However, as a proof of concept PV1 succeeded, demonstrating that the FV600 chassis possessed all the characteristics and capabilities that a HMLC needed.

When Alvis presented the concept to the War Office there was the usual 'not invented here' resistance, but as the Army was keen on the idea a General Staff Operational Requirement (GSOR) was written for a wheeled HMLC based on the concept demonstrated by PV1 and issued in April 1960. The GSOR looked closely at PV1 and indicated that various improvements were needed, including: ensuring that the cross-country performance was as good as an equivalent tracked vehicle; improving access to the mechanical elements to assist maintenance; increasing crew comfort to reduce driver fatigue, providing a flat load bay; and lowering the internal and external noise. PV1 was then shipped to FVRDE at Chertsey for trials.

The second prototype, PV2, was designed as a result of Alvis's experiences with PV1, along with the findings from the trials, and led to improvements in all areas of the original vehicle. For the vehicle to be truly amphibious, waterproofing of the cab was needed, visibility while moving in water

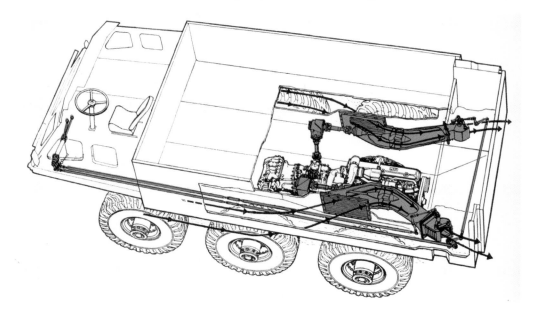

The Stalwart had a water-jet propulsion system driven from the main engine. This was needed to allow it to wade in the sea or to cross fast-flowing rivers.

had to be improved and finally a dedicated water-propulsion system needed to be designed and integrated. The cab was redesigned without doors, solving the main area for leaks, and access was via two large hatches in the roof. Forward visibility was improved with a large rectangular splash guard fitted to the front of the cab and a pair of Saro-Gill two-stage water jets driven from the gearbox were fitted, one each side to propel the vehicle while in the water.

The load bay needed to be flat and this required a redesign of the cooling system to move the radiator from its central position, from which it intruded into the load bay to the rear of the chassis, and the repositioning of the engine air intake. The Salamander's engine was a high-power version of the B81 and needed higher octane petrol than the Army's standard, so a detuned version of the B81 was fitted to PV2, a Mark 8D, which produced 213bhp at a limited 3,750rpm. The Wilson preselector gearbox was also changed to a five-speed manual all-synchromesh Meadows unit, which enabled the use of engine braking and improved the cross-country performance. The differential was a 'no spin' device to ensure that traction was not lost if a wheel was off the ground or in mud. The overall gear ratio was reduced, limiting the top speed to around 45mph (72km/h), but again improving cross-country performance.

The final major change was to the brakes. The Saladin's ring brakes were a technological dead end and the drums of the Saracen and Salamander would be overloaded in the Stalwart, so the braking system was brought fully up to date with the fitting of solid disc brakes to all six wheels. An expanding band type of handbrake that operated on the front wheels was also fitted.

PV2 was completed by the end of 1960 and underwent trials with FVRDE during 1961. In August 1961, a further nine pre-production vehicles were ordered for additional trials. Prototype PV2 was sent to Sweden at the end of 1961 for assessment by the Swedish armed forces in order to see if Stalwart could supply a series of offshore gun batteries. The trial was a success and led to an order for six production Stalwarts.

Prototype Stalwart PV3 was being built while PV2 was undergoing its UK trials and various changes were made to the specification, including a towing hitch, two roof hatches (as seen on the production versions) and an automatic gearbox from American manufacturer Allison. The extensive trials revealed a number of issues: the gearbox was not suited to the vehicle, sapping power and shifting badly; the engine had cooling issues; the brakes were inadequate; and the Saro-Gill water-drive units were not particularly efficient.

PV4 and PV5 were in build by then, so were modified with an updated cooling system, new Dowty water-propulsion units and a reversion back to the Meadows manual gearbox. A problem with the Tracta universal joints, which was causing them to fail after the vehicle had been swimming, was tracked down to water ingress via the driveshaft breather valves. A change in valve design solved the problem. The drop-down sides of the load bay caused some head scratch-

The Stalwart carried a folding swimming guard on its front panel. When deployed, it deflected water away from the front of the cab, giving the driver visibility by stopping the bow wave going over the windscreen and the top of the cab.

ing, as the company strove to find a construction that was light and strong enough, eventually settling on glass-fibre surface panels over a cellular aluminium core with an aluminium surround. This construction also gave a good base to which to fix a rubber (later neoprene) seal to ensure that the load bay was kept as dry as possible while swimming.

Stalwart Description

The production Stalwart was very similar to the PV3 and PV4 prototypes, which had been thoroughly tested by the Army before the production specification was finalized. It was fitted with a rear-mounted Rolls-Royce B81 Mark 8B engine, which was governed to 3,750rpm, where it produced 213bhp and 312lb ft of torque at 2,400rpm. The gearbox was a five-speed, manual Meadows unit, which was fitted with two belt-driven take-off points to power the two Dowty water jets, one each side. These water jets were is essence a propeller in a duct, with the front of the duct positioned just in front of the rear wheels and the outlets positioned on the outer rear corners of the hull. Top speed in the water was 4.5knots (8.3km/h). Adjustable flaps on the end of the exit nozzles allowed the water jet to be deflected, giving a steering function. They were operated by a pair of levers to the left of the driver. The rest of the drive system was the same as the other vehicles in the range, with the exception

Like the rest of the FV600 family, the Stalwart's six-wheel drive system gave it excellent cross-country performance in tough conditions.

of the fitting of disc brakes on all six wheels. These had the double advantages of giving more braking power and recovering efficiency much quicker than drums after immersion in water.

The hull had to be waterproof and able to give enough buoyancy for the vehicle to float, so had to be fully watertight. It was made from unarmoured BS968 fusion welding standard high tensile steel plates, which were fine wire carbon dioxide welded construction using BS968 steel plate. The hull was protected from corrosion by a zinc-rich primer and epoxy paint. The load bay was flat and had fold-down side plates; at the rear of the vehicle was a 'bustle', essentially a waterproof box structure that closed off the end of the load bay and allowed air to exit upwards from the rear-mounted radiator.

On the front of the cab was mounted the swim board, which was designed to deflect water away from the front of the cab – without it, the bow wave would overwhelm the front of the cabin, leaving the driver with very limited visibility. The board was carried on the front panel, under the windscreen, and when deployed had to be unfolded and swung out, then held in place with a pair of struts that connected the top edge to the top of the cab above the windscreen. Deploying the screen on the Mark 1 was a fiddly job and required a crew member to disembark to carry out the job.

A Mark 2 Stalwart was developed as the Mark 1 entered service. The Mark 2 was designated FV622 and had a number of improvements and modifications to improve cab layout so as to improve driver visibility, beef up the brakes and fit a winch to give a self-recovery capability. The Mark 2 was accepted by the British Army in 1966, with 400 ordered. The first production model was delivered during June 1966, with deliveries starting during 1967.

The Mark 2 Stalwart was produced from 1966 and was easily distinguished from the Mark 1 by its new front side windows and outer windscreens, all of which extended downward below the line of the rear cab window to improve driver visibility. Many of the modifications were made to the cabin to improve driver visibility from the central driving position, including the new front windows and the deletion of a partition to the right of the driver that covered the batteries. This was replaced with a third seat, while the batteries were relocated. A new instrument panel afforded some ergonomic advancement over the old panel; a hot water system for cooking and making a brew was fitted; and the

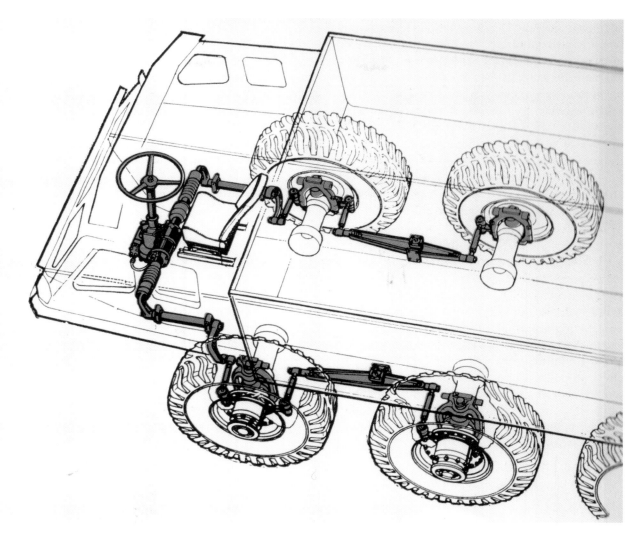

As with all of the FV600, the steering system operated on the front four wheels to increase mobility and manoeuvrability.

brakes were revised with a second master cylinder and a new Air Pac servo to reduce pedal pressure and increase efficiency.

The swim board was modified to enable the crew to unfold it and place it into position from the top hatches. In order to give adequate clearance when being loaded into the standard RAF cargo plane, the Lockheed Hercules, the front corners of the load bay front bulkhead could be unbolted and removed. The relatively high maintenance load of the Mark 1 was reduced by the use of a central lubrication system to feed oil to the driveshafts, using a circular cross member in the hull to act as an oil reservoir. The water jets

were uprated to produce 2,200lb (998kg) of thrust, increasing water speed to 5.3knots (10km/h). Finally, a self-recovery capability was achieved by the fitment of a Boughton winch and cable system, which was placed in a waterproof compartment under the cab and hydraulically powered from the engine.

The first variant of the Stalwart family was the FV623 Artillery Limber Vehicle, which was a development of the basic Stalwart and was designed to resupply tanks and self-propelled artillery guns with ammunition and other supplies in the field. The concept was initially based on the Mark 1 Stalwart and the prototype PV2 was modified with a hydraulic crane or lifting arm made by Swedish manufacturer HIAB, which was mounted just behind the cab at the front of the load bay. An additional four seats were fitted in the load bay for the maintenance crew. While the PV2 prototype demonstrated that the concept was sound and could be fitted to the Stalwart, the requirement was delayed as the Army was working on a standardized materials handling system that would be used across the organization. This specified the size and weight of all palletized stores, including ammunition, and would be applied to all the elements in the logistics chain, with the Stalwart being at the end of the line delivering ammunition and stores to tanks in the field.

The FV623s were delivered as part of the order for 325 Stalwart Mark 2s awarded to Alvis in 1966. It is thought that the missing FV621 designation would have been assigned to the vehicle had the original pre-palletized ammunition limber based on the Mark 1 Stalwart (FV620) prototype PV2 and fitted with the HIAB crane been ordered. However, by the time the Army had finalized its design for palletized ammunition, the Mark 2 Stalwart (FV622) was in production and hence the new version was designated FV623. The HIAB crane was replaced with a British manufactured Atlas and there were only two additional seats in the load bay.

The crane fitted to FV623 was modified to meet the next application that the Stalwart found itself performing, that of the FV624 Royal Electrical and Mechanical Engineers (REME)

Fitter's Vehicle. This was a mobile workshop and the only modification from REME's FV623 HMLC was a revision to the Atlas crane, giving it the capability for very fine adjustment to the length of the jib, so that a load such as an engine pack for an AFV could be positioned with accuracy when dropping it in an engine bay. REME's FV432-based Fitter's Vehicle, the 'Carrier, Armoured, Maintenance' in Army parlance, could only carry 3.5ton (3,556kg), while the Stalwart could carry up to 5ton (5,080kg).

Stalwart Production

At the end of 1962, an order was placed for the first 125 production FV620 Stalwarts. This included the remaining prototypes (PV6–PV11), which were subsumed into the order. After further trials and testing, in November 1964 the British Army ordered 325 FV622 Stalwart Mark 2s, with production aimed to run at twenty-four per month. Formal acceptance of the design by the Army was given in March 1965. There were 269 FV623s and 60 FV624s, all produced for the British Army. Note that the production of the Stalwart cab was subcontracted out to Motor Panels Ltd, also based in Coventry.

Export sales of the Stalwart were disappointing, due to the specialist nature of the machine. There were eight FV620

Rivers and the ocean could both be mastered by the Stalwart's amphibious capability.

The Scorpion reconnaissance and fire support vehicle was the first of the Combat Vehicle, Reconnaissance (Tracked) or CVR(T), or FV100 family of vehicles. With a Jaguar XK engine producing some 195bhp and a lightweight aluninium alloy hull, the FV100 had a good turn of speed. Here, the author's wife and sister-in-law are experiencing the Scorpion's performance.

Mark 1s and eighteen FV622 Mark 2s delivered to Sweden, and one FV620 (Mark 1) was sold to Berliet, a French truck company that wanted to sell the Stalwart to the French military, but no orders were forthcoming. Two FV622s (Mark 2) were sold to the German military and three were sold to Austria.

THE FV100 SERIES ARMOURED FIGHTING VEHICLES

The FV100 series of vehicles, designated Combat Vehicle, Reconnaissance (Tracked) or CVR(T), was designed under the auspices of the Alvis factory, but after the firm had lost its independence and become part of British Leyland. So in one view the FV100 was a British Leyland product, but it was the last family of vehicles to have any connection to the original Alvis factory and name, was an innovative design in its own right and had an Alvis-based design team so is included in this book. The FV100 family was a range of tracked armoured vehicles that covered a number of roles, including some covered by the FV600 family and others unique to the FV100.

On its introduction, the range comprised seven variants: the FV101 Scorpion fire support vehicle; the FV102 Striker anti-tank guided missile vehicle; the FV103 Spartan, an APC;

the FV104 Samaritan armoured ambulance; the FV105 Sultan armoured command vehicle; the FV106 Samson armoured recovery vehicle; and the FV107 Scimitar 30mm cannon vehicle.

The Scorpion was still undergoing testing at the Military Vehicles and Engineering Establishment (MVEE) in the early 1980s while the author worked there. At the time, there were rumours of a Scorpion fitted with a tuned Jaguar XK engine which reached a much higher speed than the service version – three figures were mentioned. Another time a test Scorpion was involved in a crash on the road with a large lorry – the lorry was a write-off; the Scorpion has some scratches to its paintwork …

FV100 Family Development

In 1967, Alvis was awarded a contract to design and develop a new armoured vehicle, the CRV(T), initially to replace the Saladin. The vehicle was intended to be tracked rather than wheeled and to act as a fire support vehicle, so would be armed with a lighter version of the Saladin's 76mm gun, but as a tracked vehicle would have increased mobility. The vehicle's design parameters included: high manoeuvrability; air portability; low cost; day and night operation; minimal load impact on the crew; and the capability of operating in differ-

The FV100 had three distinct hull types. This is the Spartan APC variant with a higher hull line and no turret.

The rear view of a Spartan shows the rear door and the five main wheels, plus the commander's multi-vision cupola on the top of the hull.

ent parts of the globe. The result was a small tracked vehicle with a laden weight of just 17,500lb (7,938kg), which compared very favourable with the outgoing Saladin's 25,536lb (11,583kg).

To achieve these design objectives, the FV100 family had a virtually unique feature – the use of aluminium alloy to form the hull. This had a number of advantages over the traditional steel plate armour and was made possible by advances in metallurgy which resulted in the production of aluminium alloys that offered good armour protection against small arms and artillery fragments. These offered good armour protection against small arms and artillery fragments. While the CVR(T) was the first tracked AFV with a hull made from aluminium alloy to enter service with the British armed forces, it was not the first worldwide – that honour went to the US Army's Ford-designed M113 APC, which entered service in the early 1960s and saw extensive combat service in Vietnam and elsewhere.

Design and development of the FV100 family of vehicles went smoothly, especially when viewed from today's legacy of defence contracts that have overrun in terms of budget and time. With the project starting in 1967, Alvis produced thirty prototypes, which were up and running and undergoing trials by 1970. With a production contract awarded to Alvis in 1970 for 275 Scorpions, the first vehicles entered service with the British Army in 1973 and served with the Blues and Royals.

Four Scorpions and four Scimitars served in the Falklands War in 1982 with the Blues and Royals, and most versions served in the first Gulf War in 1990.

One development of the Scorpion that Alvis had little to do with was its adoption as the AFV of choice for Palitoy's 'Action Man', the army doll much beloved of small boys during the 1970s and 1980s. Available between 1972 and 1983, the model was not quite to the correct scale, but with enough room for a commander in the turret and a driver up front.

FV100 Family Hull and Running Gear

The FV100 family shared the same lower hull, running gear and front layout. The alloy hull was designed to give the most protection in a 30-degree arc in the front of the hull and then at least 1in (25.4mm) over the rest of the structure.

There were three hull types used in the FV100 family. Scorpion (FV101) and Scimitar (FV107) had the first type, with a low hull line with turret. The Striker (FV102), Spartan (FV103) and Samson (FV106) had a higher rear hull, with a smooth sloping front extending about one-third of the length of the vehicle and a flat top to the hull for the last two-thirds of the length. The Samaritan (FV104) and Sultan (FV105) had an even higher rear hull top, with the front slope increasing after the driver's hatch to give more internal room to the hull. Suspension was by transverse torsion bar, giving around 8in (203mm) deflection and 4in (102mm) rebound. There were five light alloy road wheels on each side of the hull, fitted with solid rubber tyres that were bonded to the wheels. The tracks were light steel multi-link

Equipped with a development of the 76mm gun as used in the Saladin, the Scorpion fulfilled several roles in the British Army.

construction, with seventy-nine links per track, and were fitted with rubber bushes between the links and solid rubber road pads.

The engine was a militarized Jaguar XK 6-cylinder dohc unit, with a capacity of 4.2 litres. Running on petrol, the car-derived engine produced a healthy 195bhp at 4,750rpm, giving the Scorpion an outstanding performance with a top speed of around 50mph (80km/h). The engine was fitted in the front of the hull on the right-hand side, next to the driver's compartment, and was placed longitudinally but back to front when compared with its automobile application. The engine retained its standard wet-sump lubrication system. The engine was connected to a TN15 Crossdrive drive unit

mounted in the nose of the hull, which gave drive to the two front track sprockets. The TN15 Crossdrive gearbox was a semi-automatic epicyclic transmission, which gave seven forward and reverse gears and also provided a Merritt-Brown brake-operated steering differential. All brakes, both steering and braking, were discs.

FV101 Scorpion Fire Support Vehicle

The Scorpion was the original member of the FV100 family and was a reconnaissance and fire support vehicle, used to provide point defence and offensive capability. The 76mm

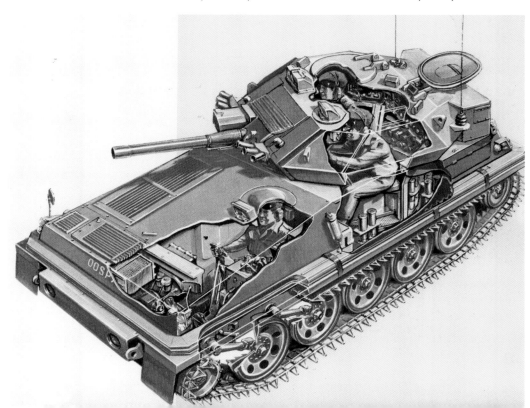

This cutaway diagram shows the internal layout of the Scorpion. The turret is set far back on the rear of the hull. The hull is relatively low so as to keep the centre of gravity and profile as low as possible.

gun was mounted in a 360-degree rotatable turret mounted on the rear of the hull top, with elevation of up to 35 degrees and depression of up to 10 degrees.

The gun was sited using a coaxial 7.62mm machine gun. The gun was able to fire high-explosive squash head (HESH) rounds for use against armoured vehicles, high-explosive rounds for use against soft-skinned vehicles and artillery pieces, as well as smoke and illumination rounds. It was supplied with a built-in river-crossing screen that enabled it to swim at around 4.4mph (7km/h) with no preparation, apart from raising the screen. Up to forty rounds of ammunition were carried internally and a crew of three comprised commander, gunner and driver.

FV102 Striker Anti-Tank Guided Missile Vehicle

The Striker was designed to provide long-range anti-tank capability using Swingfire guided missiles. It was based on a modified FV103 hull and carried up to five Swingfire missiles in a launcher mounted on the rear of the hull. The launcher comprised a rectangular box with five square missile housings and was hinged on its rear edge. When stowed, the launcher lay flat in a recess in the hull top to provide some armour protection and when firing the launcher was raised some 30–40 degrees to give the missiles clearance over the vehicle. Additional missiles were stored internally and the crew of three comprised a commander, missile controller and driver.

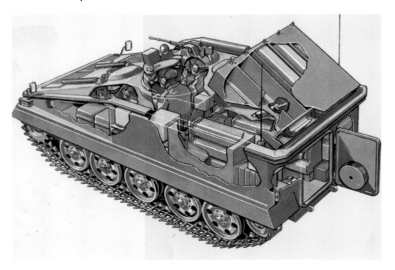

This cutaway diagram shows the internal layout of the Striker. The anti-tank guided missile silo on the rear of the hull is shown raised in its firing position.

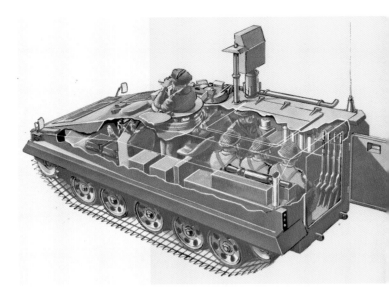

This cutaway diagram shows the internal layout of the Spartan APC. With room for only five troops, the Spartan was used to transport specialist squads into the battle zone.

FV103 Spartan Armoured Personnel Carrier

The Spartan was a small APC that shared its hull profile with the Striker and could carry five troops in its rear compartment, with access via a rear side-hinged door or through a hatch in the compartment roof. There was room for three troops sitting on the left-hand side, a fourth a in rearward-facing seat on the right-hand side and the troop commander's position facing forward in front on the right-hand side. The vehicle commander's position was on the left front of the rear compartment and was fitted with an all-round vision cupola. A 7.62 general purpose machine gun could be fitted to the cupola and fired from under armour.

FV104 Samaritan Armoured Ambulance

The Samaritan was designed as an armoured ambulance to accommodate a range of casualties. While based on the Spartan APC, the Samaritan had the hull roof raised by 12in (305mm). Permutations of casualties were four stretcher cases, two stretcher cases and three sitting cases, or six sitting cases. In addition to these casualties, a single medical orderly was carried and a second orderly or single sitting case could also be accommodated. The vehicle had a crew of two, driver and commander.

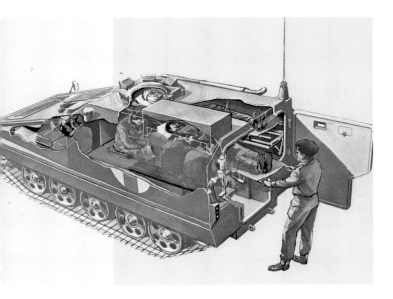

This cutaway diagram shows the internal layout of the Samaritan ambulance. With room for up to four stretcher cases, or a mixture of casualties and orderlies, the Samaritan, along with the Sultan, had the highest hull profile.

FV105 Sultan Armoured Command Vehicle

The Sultan was designed as an armoured command vehicle and shared its hull with the Samaritan. Fitted with a full set of command post radios, the vehicle also had an extending tent permanently fixed to the rear of the vehicle to provide additional accommodation. With a crew of three, commander, driver and radio operator, the Sultan could also house an additional two or three crew members in the hull.

FV106 Samson Armoured Recovery Vehicle

The Samson was an armoured recovery vehicle and used the same hull as the Spartan, with the rear compartment given over to a heavy duty winch, which had a rated maximum pull of 13.5ton (13,716kg). A triangular ground anchor was fitted to the rear, which hinged down to dig into the ground while winching. An appliqué propeller kit was also available to improve the Samson's swimming capability. The Samson had a crew of three, commander, driver and winch operator.

This cutaway diagram shows the internal layout of the Sultan command vehicle. The extending tent on the rear of the vehicle gave additional space for HQ staff.

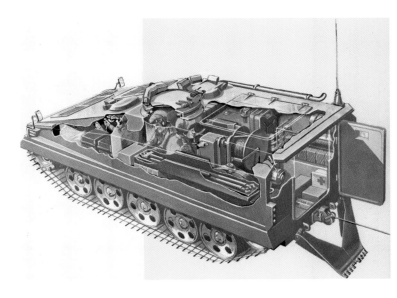

This cutaway diagram shows the internal layout of the Samson armoured recovery vehicle. The rear compartment housed a winch used to extract other vehicles from sticky situations.

SPECIFICATION TABLE: AFVS – SALADIN, STALWART, SCORPION AND SPARTAN

	Saladin	Stalwart Mk 2
Engine		
Type	Rolls-Royce B80 Mk 6D	Rolls-Royce B81 Mk 8B/2
Crankcase and Block	One piece cast iron	One piece cast iron
Head	Cast iron	Cast iron
Cylinders	Eight in line	Eight in line
Cooling	Water	Water
Bore and Stroke	88.9 x 114.3mm	95.2 x 114.3mm
Capacity	5,765 cc	6516 cc
Valves	Two per cylinder	Inlet over exhaust
Compression Ratio	6.4:1	6.5:1
Max power	160bhp at 3,750rpm	220bhp at 4,000rpm
Transmission		
Gearbox	Five-speed, pre-selector type	Five-speed
Clutch	Fluid coupling	Single plate Borg and Beck
Suspension		
All Six Wheels	Independent, coil spring and wishbone, articulated drive shafts	Independent, coil spring and wishbone, articulated drive shafts
Brakes		
Type	Ring type brakes	Lockheed discs on all wheels
Dimensions		
Length	193in (4.9m)	250in (6.4m)
Width	101in (2.515m)	103in (2.62m)
Height	94in (2.39m)	102in (2.6m)
Track	82in (2.03m)	80.5in (2.04m)
Wheelbase	120in (3.05m)	120in (3.05m)
Weight	23,072lb (10,500kg)	23,184lb (10,515kg)

	Scorpion	Spartan
Engine		
Type	Jaguar XK DOHC	Jaguar XK DOHC
Crankcase and Block	One piece cast iron	One piece cast iron
Head	Cast alloy	Cast alloy
Cylinders	Six in line	Six in line
Cooling	Water	Water
Bore and Stroke	92.08 x 106mm	92.08 x 106mm
Capacity	4,235cc	4,235cc
Valves	Two per cylinder	Two per cylinder
Compression Ratio	Not known	Not known
Max power	195bhp at 4,750rpm	195bhp at 4,750rpm

(continued opposite)

(continued from previous page)

	Scorpion	Spartan
Transmission		
Gearbox	7 Speed N15x Crossdrive semi automatic	7 Speed N15x Crossdrive semi automatic
Clutch	Centrifugal	Centrifugal
Suspension	Transverse torsion bars, 5 per side	Transverse torsion bars, 5 per side
Brakes		
Type	Discs	Discs
Dimensions		
Length	187.5in (475.9cm)	187.5in (475.9cm)
Width	86in (218.4cm)	86in (218.4cm)
Height	82.5in (209.6cm)	79.5in (201.6cm)
Track Centres	5 ft 7in (170.8cm)	67in (170.8cm)
Weight	38580lb (17,500kg)	37,467lb (16,995kg)

FV107 Scimitar 30mm Cannon Vehicle

The Scimitar was an armoured reconnaissance vehicle, designed to carry out reconnaissance and security roles while retaining a capability to defeat light armoured vehicles. It was virtually identical to the Scorpion, but had a 30mm Rarden cannon fitted in a modified turret mantlet, replacing the 76mm gun and coaxial machine gun. A crew of three, commander, driver and gunner, was carried.

The FV100 Legacy

The FV100 has been a success for Alvis and the subsequent owners of the name. Some 1,500 units were supplied to the British armed forces and the vehicle was particularly successful as an export, being sold to some twenty-two countries. Total FV100 production was over 3,000 units, the majority of them being Scorpions.

While the CVR(T) first entered service in the late 1960s, at the time of writing vehicles in the FV100 family are still in service with the British Army and in other armed forces around the world. The British Army still uses the Scimitar as a reconnaissance vehicle, as well as the Spartan APC, the Samaritan armoured ambulance, the Sultan armoured command vehicle and the Sampson recovery vehicle, albeit

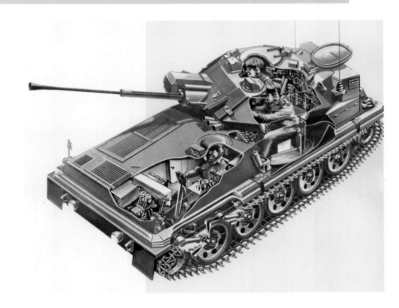

This cutaway diagram shows the internal layout of the Scimitar. Similar to the Scorpion, the Scimitar's turret was adapted to carry a 30mm quick-firing cannon.

in re-engined forms with Cummins diesel engines. Still in use over four decades after they first entered service, the FV100 family has served the British armed forces well and is a lasting testament to the skills and expertise of the Alvis engineers who designed the vehicles.

CHAPTER TEN

POST-WAR
AERO ENGINES

INTRODUCTION

As described in Chapter 5, Alvis's pre-World War II foray into aero-engine production floundered amidst contractural problems, but it did give the company a good grounding in aero-engine production and the company's ability to work in the aero-engine industry was fully vindicated by its sterling work carried out rebuilding aero engines during World War II. After the disappointment of the Gnome-Rhône issues, in 1938 Alvis had started to design a single-row radial of its own design, which would come to be called the Leonides and was designed to compete in the 500hp range. This design would also lead to the 14-cylinder, twin-row radial, the Leonides Major.

In the late 1940s, Alvis also recognized the importance of the emerging helicopter market and designed mounting packs for both versions of the Leonides, which incorporated

a cooling fan and clutch mechanism that could be mounted vertically, horizontally or at all points in-between.

The only problem was that by the time the Leonides family of engines was going into production in the late 1940s, the gas-turbine engine was maturing rapidly and would soon be a significant competitor, with higher power to weight ratios than the piston engine could ever hope to achieve. As an example, the Napier Gazelle, the first British gas-turbine engine designed for fitment in a helicopter and produced from the mid-1950s, gave 1,465 shaft horsepower and weighed around 830lb (376.5kg), compared with the Leonides Major's 850bhp and weight of some 1,200lb (544kg). The figures tell the whole story – the days of the piston engine were limited.

A contract for the development of a new radial engine in the 750bhp class was given to Alvis by the Air Ministry

One of the most common applications for the Alvis Leonides aero engine was the Hunting Percival Provost. Taken from the Alvis brochure, this representation shows a Provost in action.

The Leonides was also used in helicopters, where it was installed with the crankshaft aligned vertically. A large cooling fan and clutch mechanism was positioned on the top of the engine.

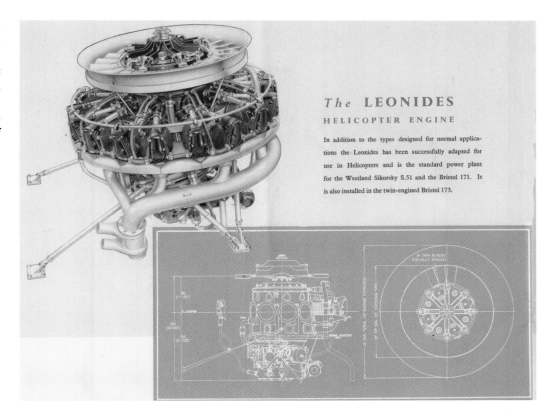

The LEONIDES
HELICOPTER ENGINE

In addition to the types designed for normal applications the Leonides has been successfully adapted for use in Helicopters and is the standard power plant for the Westland Sikorsky S.51 and the Bristol 171. It is also installed in the twin-engined Bristol 173.

in 1951. The specification asked for an engine that would be suitable for use in helicopters and aircraft, so capable of being at any angle between horizontal and vertical. The result was the Leonides Major, a 14-cylinder two-row radial, which, while sharing its layout and many design features with the original Leonides, was very much not just a doubled-up version. The engine was aimed at two applications – four were to be fitted to the soon to be announced Handley Page Herald feeder liner and also to the Royal Navy's Westland Whirlwind HAS.7. While the engine made it into production in the Whirlwind, it was never fitted into any fixed-wing aircraft and in the Whirlwind proved to be less than satisfactory. The first two Herald prototypes flew with four Leonides Majors, but the production versions were powered by a pair of Rolls-Royce Dart turbo props – another example of the gas turbine taking over from the piston engine.

Production of the Leonides and Leonides Major was limited and over the eighteen-year production run (1947–65), a total of just over 2,000 complete Leonides units were produced, with production peaking in 1955 at just under 300 units. There were about 270 Leonides Majors manufactured during the 1950s.

The last Leonides came off the production line in 1965. Alvis continued to support its engines up to 1988, when the last Percival Pembrokes left service with the British armed forces. Further aviation work for the aero-engine factory came from a contract to overhaul Avco Lycoming's 4-, 6- and 8-cylinder engines, but this work had virtually gone by the late 1970s, so the end of the support work for the Pembroke signified the end of Alvis's involvement in the aviation business.

TECHNICAL DESCRIPTION OF THE LEONIDES AND LEONIDES MAJOR

The Leonides was a single-row 9-cylinder air-cooled radial engine with two pushrod-operated valves per cylinder. It was equipped with a single-speed, single-stage supercharger and a fuel-injection system. With a bore and stroke of 122 × 112mm, the unit displaced 11780cc (just under the 12-litre limit imposed on the company by Gnome-Rhône) and with a compression ratio of 6.8:1 gave a maximum power of 545bhp

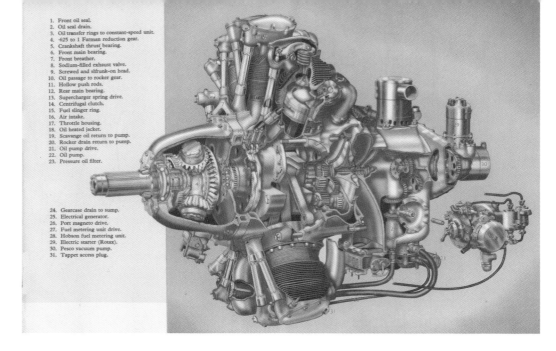

The Leonides was a 9-cylinder single-row air-cooled radial engine. This cutaway diagram shows the major components and the layout of the engine.

at 3,000rpm, with supercharger boost pressure of 6.5lb per square inch. Later versions had their stroke increased to 122mm, giving a capacity of 12831cc and a maximum power of 650bhp at 3,200rpm.

The crankcase was made from a pair of light alloy castings that were split vertically, giving (in conventional aircraft applications) a front and rear element. A propeller reduction gear casting was bolted to the front crankcase, which contained a 0.625:1 Farman type reduction gear, and a diffuser casting was bolted to the rear crankcase. This casing housed vertical and horizontal ancillary driveshafts, all driven from the crank. A single-track roller main bearing was fitted in each half to support the crankshaft and the front case was extended in front of the main bearing to carry roller type tappets to operate the pushrods and to carry the timing gear. The crankshaft was a single throw type, was supported on two main bearings and was made in two halves, with the split on the centre line of the crankpin, with a splined coupling pin passing through the centre of the crankpin, which was secured in place with a clamping bolt. The connecting-rod assembly comprised a master rod and eight articulated rods, with the master rod operating cylinder number 6. The master rod rotated on the crankpin and the articulated rods were attached to lugs on the master rod by wrist pins.

The pistons were light alloy castings and were attached to the connecting rods by floating gudgeon pins held in place with circlips. Each had three rings – two top rings for compression and the lower one for oil control. The individual cylinder barrels were made of nitrided steel and were bolted on to the crankcase on their base flange; each light alloy head

was screwed and shrunk on to its barrel. Each individual cylinder and head was extensively finned to ensure adequate engine cooling.

The valves were operated from a pair of cam rings mounted on the front of the engine and driven at half the crankshaft speed through timing gears. Each track had four lobes, which operated on a roller cam follower mounted in the crankcase to transmit the cam's movement to the individual pushrods, then up the valves. Each valve was operated by a rocker that ran on a ball bearing on its shaft and was held close by coil springs. The exhaust valves were sodium filled for cooling.

The engine's oil system had three circuits: the main pressure circuit, which fed the main and big-end bearings, along with the undersides of the pistons and gear in the crankcases; the main scavenge circuit, which returned the oil to the sump; and the rocker-box scavenge circuit. Each circuit had its own oil pump, which was bolted together and mounted on the diffuser casting at the rear of the engine and was powered from the bottom of the vertical driveshaft.

The supercharger was fitted at the rear of the engine and was a single-stage centrifugal type that fed through a twelve-vane diffuser to the delivery chamber, which was formed between the rear crankcase casting and the diffuser casing. Ignition was provided by a pair of BTH magnetos mounted on the diffuser casing, which were driven from the shafts mounted in the diffuser casing.

The fuel-injection system had a Hobson type A.L.1 fuel metering unit and throttle body, with a Hobson Mark 53 boost controller. The throttle body was oil-heated and

ABOVE: **This shot of the Leonides aero engine shows the alloy cylinder heads attached to iron cylinders and the exhaust ring that runs around the rear of the engine.**

RIGHT: **The Leonides Major was a 14-cylinder twin-row air-cooled radial engine. It was developed from Alvis's experiences with the Leonides and shared the same bore and stroke.**

injected fuel directly into the eye of the supercharger impeller, avoiding any icing issues with the inlet side of the engine. The inlet 'manifold' was a circular void around the rear crankcase casting and individual pipes fed the charge up to the individual cylinder head.

With all ancillaries fitted and ready for installation in a conventional aircraft, the Leonides was 52.8in (1,341mm) in length and 41.5in (1,054mm) in diameter. Alvis produced the engine as a 'power egg', with all fittings incorporated and with the engine ready to fit to an aircraft; in this form it included a close fitting and efficient cowling that added a mere 0.5in (12.7mm) to the overall diameter.

The Leonides Major was a twin-row 14-cylinder air-cooled radial engine with two pushrod-operated valves per cylinder. It was equipped with a single-speed, single-stage supercharger and a fuel-injection system. With a bore and stroke of 122 × 112mm, the unit displaced 18317cc and with a compression ratio of 6.535:1 it gave a maximum power of 870bhp at 3,000rpm, with supercharger boost pressure of 9.25lb per square inch.

The crankcase was made from three light alloy forgings that were split vertically, giving (in conventional aircraft applications) a front, centre and rear element. As with the single-row Leonides, a Farman propeller reduction gear casting was bolted to the front crankcase with 0.533:1 gearing, and a diffuser casting was bolted to the rear crankcase, which also housed the vertical and horizontal ancillary drive-shafts, all driven from the crank. A single-track roller main bearing was fitted in each of the three crankcase forgings to support the crankshaft, while the front bearing was a ball-thrust bearing that was used to locate the crankshaft.

The front and rear cases were extended in front of the main bearing to carry roller type tappets to operate the pushrods and to carry the timing gear. The crankshaft was a two-throw type, was supported on three main bearings and was made in three parts, with the join on the vertical centre line of each crankpin. The sections were fixed using two externally splined hollow couplings that passed through the centre of the crankpin and were fixed using draw bolts through each of the shafts to lock the crankshaft assembly together. The two connecting-rod assemblies comprised a one-piece master rod and six articulated rods, with the master rods operating cylinder numbers 4 and 11.

The master rod rotated on the crankpin, while the articulated rods were attached to lugs on the master rod by wrist

CLOCKWISE, FROM TOP LEFT:
Three views of the Leonides in helicopter form, showing the cooling and clutch mechanism, plus the compact dimensions of the package.

The Leonides Major packaged for helicopter applications.

The Leonides fitted into a helicopter, in this case a Bristol 171.

pins using phosphor bronze bushes. The pistons were light alloy forgings and were attached to the connecting rods by floating gudgeon pins held in place with circlips. Each had four rings – two top tapered rings for compression and below them two scraper rings for oil control. The individual cylinder barrels and heads followed the Leonides principles. The valves were operated from two pairs of cam rings mounted on the front and rear of the engine and were driven at half the crankshaft speed through timing gears. The valves and rocker gear were similar to those of the smaller Leonides.

The engine's oil system was again similar to that of the Leonides, as was the supercharger location and operation, plus the various ancillaries, including the two magnetos. With all ancillaries fitted and ready for installation in

ALVIS AERO-ENGINE SPECIFICATIONS

Type	Leonides 531 Series	Leonides 554 Series (Helicopter)	Leonides Major 702 Series	Leonides Major 750 Series (Helicopter)
Crankshaft orientation	9-cylinder single- row radial	9-cylinder single- row radial	14-cylinder two- row radial	14-cylinder two- row radial
Cooling	Horizontal Airflow	Vertical to horizontal Forced fan fed	Horizontal Airflow	Horizontal Forced fan fed
Bore and stroke	4.8 × 4.8in	4.8 × 4.8in	4.8 × 4.41in	4.8 × 4.41in
Capacity	12831cc	12831cc	18317.5cc	18317.5cc
Compression ratio	6.5:1	6.5:1	6.8:1	6.9:1
Power – max rating	650bhp @ 3,200rpm	635bhp @ 3,200rpm	885bhp @ 3,000rpm	795bhp @ 2,900rpm
Power – max continuous	590bhp @ 3,000rpm	590bhp @ 3,000rpm	750bhp @ 2,900	695bhp @ 2,900
Weight	855lb (388kg)	790lb (358kg)	1,200lb (544kg)	1,065lb (483kg)
Diameter	43in (1,092mm)	43in (1,092mm)	38.9in (988mm)	38.9in (988mm)
Length	54.5in (1,384mm)	32.8in (833mm)	62.0in (1,575mm)	54.8in (1,392mm)
Frontal area	10.1sq ft (0.938sq m)	n/a	8.2sq ft (0.762sq m)	n/a

a conventional aircraft, the Leonides Major was 70.896in (1,801mm) in length and 38.925in (988.7mm) in diameter. As with the smaller Leonides, Alvis produced the engine as a 'power egg', with all fitting incorporated and with the engine ready to fit to an aircraft.

Both the Leonides and the Leonides Major were adapted for use in helicopters. The initial helicopter packaging had the engine mounted vertically, with the oil system modified from the original design to allow for the change in orientation of the motor. There was no need for the propeller reduction mechanism, so the complete mechanism and the front casting (which would have been on top in the helicopter application) were discarded and replaced with a new casting that housed a clutch mechanism and a cooling fan, which was bolted to a coupling flange splined on to the end of the crankshaft. Circular pressed-steel ducting surrounded the fan and directed the cooling air over the cylinders and heads. The thinking behind the configuration was to keep the centre of gravity as low as possible in the installation, and when fitted to early helicopters such as the Bristol Sycamore and Westland Dragonfly, the complete unit was mounted on the floor of the craft, with the drive taken vertically up to the rotor head. Later installations, such as that on the Westland

Whirlwind, had the engine mounted in the nose at an angle, with the drive going backwards and upwards to the rotor head via a series of shafts and gearboxes.

THE LEONIDES AND LEONIDES MAJOR IN SERVICE

The Leonides and Leonides Major may not have sold many units, but they were fitted to a wide range of aircraft, both fixed- and rotary-winged, and played an important role in the development of the UK's helicopter industry. The following details all the aircraft that were powered by Alvis's aero engines.

Leonides-Powered Fixed-Wing Aircraft

After the Leonides was tested in an Avro Anson, the first conventional aircraft to be fitted with the Leonides was the Cunliffe-Owen Concordia, an attractive low-wing twin-engined ten- to twelve-seat feeder airliner. The first two engines were delivered to Cunliffe-Owen in 1947, with the

The Leonides was fitted to the RAF's primary trainer, the Provost, which was in service from 1953.

prototype taking to the air in May of that year. A second prototype was completed and flew in late 1947, but no orders were forthcoming and the project was cancelled in 1948.

The first major user of the Alvis aero engine was Hunting Percival, which used two Leonides engines to power its P50 Prince, which first flew in 1948. The Prince was a twin-engined high-wing feeder airliner that could carry up to ten passengers. It was developed into the Sea Prince to meet the Royal Navy's need for navigation and anti-submarine warfare training and was also used in a transport role. The Prince was developed into the P66 Pembroke with a larger wing to permit a better load-carrying capability. It first flew in 1952 and entered service with the RAF in 1953, where it replaced the venerable Avro Anson for light transport duties. It was also produced as the Pembroke C(PR), a photo-reconnaissance variant. The last Pembrokes finally left service in 1988.

The second Hunting Percival aircraft to have the Leonides fitted was the P56 Provost. This single-engined low-wing two-seater was designed in accordance with the RAF's need for a basic trainer that reflected the higher performance of its jet-powered operational fighters and bombers. While the first two prototypes were powered with Armstrong Siddeley Cheetah radial engines and first flew in 1950, the third prototype and all 461 production aircraft were powered by the Leonides. Hunting Percival later developed the Provost into the Jet Provost with an Armstrong Siddeley Viper, which first flew in 1954, only a year after the first piston-engined Provosts entered service. The Jet Provost entered service in 1958, while the last Provosts were retired from their training role in the early 1960s.

Scottish Aviation was based in Prestwick, Scotland, and produced two production aircraft powered by the Leonides engine. The single-engined Pioneer was a light, high-wing single-engined aircraft, with the ability to operate from short and rough strips. With a large wing, the Pioneer first flew in 1947, powered by a de Havilland Gypsy Queen engine, and showed great Short Take-Off and Landing (STOL) performance. However, the company received no orders, so produced a Series II version in 1950 that sported a Leonides engine. This did spark some market interest and about fifty-nine Pioneers were produced, with the majority going to the RAF, where their STOL characteristics were put to good use supporting the Army in various overseas actions. The Twin Pioneer, as the name implies, was a twin-engined STOL high-wing cargo plane and first flew in 1955. Again, the majority of the eighty-seven Twin Pioneers made were supplied to the RAF, although five, powered by Pratt & Whitney radials, were supplied to Philippine Air Lines.

Still flying with the Shuttleworth Collection, this Provost was undergoing an engine overhaul at the time of writing.

Prototypes or one-off aircraft fitted with Alvis Leonides engines include: the SB2 variant of the Shorts SA6 Sealand II twin-engined high-wing flying boat; the single-engined Argentinian DL 22 Trainer; the de Havilland Beaver Series 2; the Canadian Husky F11 single-engined bush aircraft; Spain's CASA C210 Alcotán twin-engined feeder liner; and Italy's four-engined Augusta AZ8L medium-range airliner. None progressed further than a single prototype.

The Leonides Major was only fitted to two fixed-wing aircraft, the first being a twin-engined Miles Marathon designated HPR5, which was used as a test bed, and the second was the two prototype Handley Page HPR3 Heralds, each of which had four Leonides Major units fitted. Production Heralds were fitted with two Napier Dart turboprop engines.

Leonides-Powered Rotary-Wing Aircraft

The Fairey Gyrodyne was fitted with a Leonides in 1948, when it made the Class G international speed record for rotary-wing aircraft, a first helicopter speed record for Britain. Despite the Gyrodyne being a hybrid helicopter, it was fitted with a standard horizontally mounted Leonides.

The Bristol Sycamore (Type 171) was Bristol's first helicopter and the first two prototypes were powered by the Pratt & Whitney Wasp Junior, flying in 1947. The third prototype, the 171 Mark 2, first flew in September 1949 and was powered by a vertical 'helicopter' specification Leonides. From this came the first production variant, the Type 171 Mark 3, twenty-three of which were produced from 1949 and all of which were powered by the Leonides. Examples of these were used by the RAF from 1953. The Leonides-powered Sycamore Mark 4 was introduced in 1953, with 154 produced in total.

The twin-rotor Bristol Type 173 was first flown in 1952, powered by two Leonides motors as used in the Sycamore. The rotor boxes were interconnected with a shaft and the engines were equipped with a clutch mechanism, so if one engine stopped the other would continue to drive both rotors. Built in small numbers, the Type 173 was used to develop the technology needed to produce twin-rotor heavy lift helicopters and the Leonides Major powered the later Bristol 173/3, 173/4, 173/5 and 191/1 variants. The RAF's first twin-rotor helicopter, the Bristol Belvedere, was developed from this range and were powered by the Napier Gazelle gas-turbine unit.

The helicopter version of the Alvis Leonides engine was used to power the first hovercraft – the Saunders-Roe SR-N1 of 1959.

The Percival Prince small airliner and Bristol 171 helicopter were powered by the Leonides engine.

The Royal Navy's Westland Dragonfly helicopter and the Percival Sea Prince navigation and anti-submarine warfare trainer and transport seen here were both powered by the Leonides.

The Alvis aero-engine venture was the right product at the wrong time, as by the time Alvis engines were in production the jet age had arrived. This de Havilland Goblin is a first-generation engine that went into production during World War II.

Based in Yeovil, Somerset, in the UK, Westland followed Bristol's lead and entered the helicopter market in 1947, when it signed a licensing agreement with the US company United Aircraft Corporation. This gave Westland access to the design of the Sikorsky S51, which in Westland's hands was called the Dragonfly. Replacing much of the American design's equipment, including the engine, with British-designed and manufactured items, the Dragonfly gave Westland its first helicopter and laid the foundation for further cooperation and licensing of Sikorsky designs, resulting in the Whirlwind, Wessex and Sea King. The first UK-built Dragonfly flew in 1948 and was powered by an Alvis Leonides 50 engine producing 520bhp. The Dragonfly could carry up to four crew and served in the Royal Navy in the air-sea rescue 'plane guard' role, and with the RAF mainly in the casualty evacuation role. Civilian versions were also produced, serving with airlines BEA and Silver City, and it was bought by various other companies as a general purpose machine. A total of 149 Dragonflies were produced. Those in service in the UK armed forces were withdrawn from service in the early 1950s, when they were often replaced with Whirlwinds.

The Westland Widgeon was a development of the Dragonfly, with the cabin modified to provide an extra seat. It was fitted with a Leonides 521/2 engine producing 520bhp. First flying in 1955, only fifteen Widgeons were produced, with three being converted to Dragonflies and the rest were new builds. The helicopters were used by Bristow in the Persian Gulf to service oil rigs, as well as by the Hong Kong Police, the Brazilian Navy and the Royal Jordanian Air Force.

The replacement for the Dragonfly was the Westland Whirlwind, a licence-built Sikorsky S-55, which was a larger and more capable helicopter than the Dragonfly. Planned to be powered by a Leonides Major with some 50 per cent more power than the Dragonfly's unit, the Whirlwind could carry a significantly larger load faster and further. All of the Whirlwind Series 1 variants were powered by American Pratt & Whitney radial engines, but the Series 2 machines, including the Royal Navy's first anti-submarine helicopter, the Westland Whirlwind HAS Mark 7, were powered by a 750hp Leonides Major engine. The helicopter came into service in June 1957, equipping No. 845 Squadron soon afterwards.

Unfortunately, in service the Leonides Major proved to be unreliable and after several engine-related accidents the whole Whirlwind HAS Mark 7 fleet was grounded between April and November 1959. The causes of engine failures suffered by the Leonides Major were twofold. Firstly, the engine was prone to main-bearing failure, which was caused by unexpected torsional loads imposed on the crankshaft by the transmission, resulting in whipping (uncontrolled up and down movement) of the crankshaft and failure of both the main bearings and of the central crankshaft bearing sleeve. Secondly, there were instances of failure of the clutch mechanism, which may have been caused by the main-bearing failure. The RAF bought a pair of Whirlwind HCC Mark 8s powered by the Leonides Major for the Queen's Flight, which went into service in November 1959. These HCC Mark 8s were to mark the last time the Leonides was used in a helicopter, as the piston engine was rendered obsolete by the emergence of powerful, light and reliable gas-turbine engines, with the Napier Gazelle being the first British gas-turbine engine to be designed specifically for helicopter applications.

CONCLUSION

Alvis's foray into the aero-engine market eventually ended when the gas-turbine engine took a huge proportion of the market. Unfortunately, Alvis had been too focused on the piston engine and had not envisaged the emergence of the jet engine in all its forms. The whole concept of the Leonides was close to obsolescence when it was first designed and it was quickly overwhelmed by the jet – as shown by the development of the Provost into the Jet Provost and the use of Dart turboprops on the production versions of the Herald.

Orders for the Leonides and Leonides Major ceased in 1965 and production of complete engines stopped. While Alvis did consider entering the gas-turbine market by looking at buying Blackburn Engines Ltd, which made the relatively unsuccessful Nimbus turbine engine, eventually the company pulled out of the aero-engine field. After the takeover by Rover, Alvis did pick up Rover's own gas-turbine work, that of producing small jet engines for use as auxiliary power units, but there would not be another Alvis aero engine.

CHAPTER ELEVEN

POSTSCRIPT

INTRODUCTION

This chapter ties up a few loose ends in the Alvis story. It looks at some Alvis models that never made it into production and also provides details of the very active club scene that Alvis owners and enthusiasts can access.

THE LOST ALVIS – ALEC ISSIGONIS AND THE TA175/350 PROJECT

Greek-born Sir Alec Issigonis was the designer who, while working at Morris after World War II, was responsible for the new unitary construction Minor and Oxford MO. In Feb-

Pictured at a New Year meet at Brooklands, Jonathan Huggett's TD21 convertible and behind it his 12/50.

Alvis owners are enthusiastic and enjoy formal and informal meets. Here is the Harcourt family's Duncan Coupé in a rainy Newlands Corner meet.

ruary 1952, Morris merged with Austin to become British Motor Corporation and the Austin design office appeared to be more favoured than the Morris office. Issigonis saw the writing on the wall and when a post was advertised at Alvis for a designer to take on the design and development of a new car he got the job. With a contract dated 5 June 1952, Issigonis formally joined Alvis as the head of a new design team, although reference to his notebooks shows that he was already exploring possibilities for the new car from March of that year.

Issigonis was an interesting choice for the design of a new Alvis. With his widely known views and track record on the design and production of cars for the people, as well as his dislike for 'styling' of cars, it was surprising that Alvis engaged him to design an upmarket, low-production car, a market in which technical innovation was probably less important than looks.

The new car was designated the TA 175/350 and Issigonis built a small team with mechanical engineer Chris Kingham and body engineer Harry Barbar, who brought in John Sheppard and Fred Boubier as assistants. The transmission was looked after by Bill Casseles, who was recruited from the Standard Motor Company, from whence the suspension

engineer Harry Harris was also recruited. Alex Moulton, the pioneer of the use of rubber in suspension systems, was also brought in as a consultant by Issigonis to advise on the use of rubber in the suspension.

The objective of the TA 175/350 project was to produce a car that would take Alvis forward through the 1950s and into the 1960s. The car had to be innovative and well designed, as well as being practical and offering a performance at least equal to its rivals. Power was to come from two new modular engines – a 1750cc straight-4 and a 3500cc V8. The bodyshell was to be a steel monocoque and it had to provide enough room to carry six adults in comfort, with a boot big enough for their luggage. All-round independent suspension, four doors, all-alloy engines and automatic transmission completed the picture of a thoroughly modern car. With a tight-knit and small team, the design had been clarified by the middle of 1952 and a prototype car was up and running.

The new V8's design had some problems. Originally, Issigonis insisted on a light alloy barrel type crankcase enclosing a cast-iron main-bearing support and the differential expansion of the two materials caused problems with a noisy and rattly bottom end and unwanted component movement. Power output was not great either, with a lowly and noisy 124bhp at 4,000rpm only being achieved after extensive development. The engine bottom end was eventually redesigned by Chris Kingham to a more conventional design, which quietened the engine down but did not solve the lack of power. Luckily the prototype car was fairly light and the engine produced a reasonable amount of torque, so the performance was acceptable. The engine was slotted into an all-new monocoque steel bodyshell, which featured an underslung transmission tunnel to give a flat floor and styling, all done by Issigonis, which looked a bit like an overgrown Morris Minor. The complete car was a relatively short 14ft (4,267mm) long and weighed in at a reasonable 2,576lb (1,169kg).

With a wheel at each corner, the body design followed Issigonis's quest for maximum internal space for minimal outside dimensions and was a three-box design, with four doors and a decent-sized boot. The waistline was kept low to aid visibility, the front and rear overhangs were short, there were no rear fins in order to avoid any instability in side winds, and the remit was 'the greatest possible simplicity of line' – hence the resemblance to an overgrown Morris saloon. A traditional Alvis rectangular chromed grille was the only nod to the Alvis heritage and the interior, also styled by Issigonis, was very functional and noticeably lacking in frills. The car's styling, and especially the no-frills interior, caused ructions with Alvis's marketing people, who valued the wood and leather gentleman's club-like environs of the traditional Alvis interior. Thinking of production and servicing, the body featured simple shapes to make up the panels so that production tooling could be kept as simple (read cheap) as possible and the front and rear wings were bolted on. The result was a conventional but modern looking car with an obvious resemblance to the current Morris saloon range.

Under the skin, the car's 3.5-litre V8 gave it adequate go, although whether the proposed 1750cc 4-cylinder engine would have coped cannot be known now. The transmission system featured a two-speed automatic gearbox coupled to an overdrive to give four forward gear ratios. The influence of Moulton was shown by the adoption of rubber cone springs on the all-independent suspension – probably the first automotive application of the system that would become famous in the future Mini. The suspension did not just innovate with rubber springing; the suspension units on each side of the car were interconnected using water and rubber hoses to be the first example of the Hydrolastic system.

In 1953, Alvis conducted a financial review of the project, which indicated that if the company produced around 5,000 units per annum and sold the cars for between £850 and £890, as long as the unit cost was around £590 the car could be profitable. However, the tooling and one-off costs to get the car into production would be around £650,000, and funding this expense out of the company's coffers would be difficult. Work continued, but, by 1955, while the team had managed to produce a 3.5-litre running prototype that was being tested, the finances behind the project were causing more concern. With the realization that projected sales would probably be around 5,000 units per annum, body manufacturer Pressed Steel raised its original cost estimate by a significant amount, as its original estimate had been based on 10,000 units per annum. In addition to this blow, the overall costs for Alvis to tool up for production were increasing as well. Alvis as a company did not have enough cash reserves to fund the costs of getting the car into production without outside help. The company's bankers finally killed off the project by refusing to underwrite a loan to cover the costs, so the plug was pulled in June 1955. This meant that the TA 175/350 project was dead and the design team was disbanded.

With the cancellation of the project Issigonis left Alvis and returned to BMC in 1955, where he would go on to produce what was probably his finest and most recognized design – the Mini.

RESURRECTION BY ROVER

There were two postscripts to the end of Alvis as a car producer. The Rover takeover of 1965 resulted in a design study by Rover stylist David Bache for a two-door fastback version of the Rover P6 that would have been badged the Alvis GTS. Rover also produced a prototype V8-powered mid-engined coupé, the P6BS, which was unveiled in 1968 and had a lot of Alvis engineering input and was built at the Alvis plant.

Alvis GTS

The Alvis GTS was an attempt to capitalize on the Alvis name and reputation and to produce a replacement for the ageing TF21. Designed and styled by David Bache and with a single prototype produced, the Alvis GTS was based on the

The Alvis GTS and Rover P6BS were both produced after Alvis was bought by Rover. Both were proposed to be badged as Alvis, but never made it into production.

The Alvis GTS was based on the Rover P6 saloon.

The GTS interior borrowed from the Rover parts bin, but also displayed some new designs, like the instrument cluster, which would appear on later Rovers.

The **GTS** was a three-door hatchback design. The high rear lip added rigidity, a feature that would be seen in the later **Rover SD1**.

Rover P6 platform. It was a neatly styled fastback two-door coupé with room for four passengers and, unusually for the time, an opening hatchback. A single prototype was built by the London-based coachbuilder Radford and was based on a Rover P6 2000S – an early sports version of the standard 2000 that did not make it into production.

The GTS had the Rover's fully up to date underpinnings, with Rover's new 2-litre ohc engine giving around 90bhp. Front suspension was independent and was in effect an unequal length wishbone layout, but with the top wishbone turned through 90 degrees, so that it pivoted from the scuttle. This gave plenty of room in the engine bay, which was originally designed in the P6 to have enough room to fit a gas-turbine engine.

While the dampers were located conventionally on the top link, the springs were mounted horizontally behind the top link and operated by pushrods. The equally complex rear suspension had a pair of trailing arms to locate the hubs in the fore and aft plane, fixed-length driveshafts that located the hubs transversely, coil springs with concentric dampers and a sliding variable track de Dion tube to keep the wheels parallel to each other. The de Dion tube was filled with oil to ensure friction-free movement and was located by a pair of links that ran from the outer top of the tube back to the bodywork behind the rear wheels. Disc brakes were fitted

all round, with the rears mounted inboard close to the differential.

The GTS's bonnet has a pair of bulges in it, which indicates that the fitment of a Rover V8 engine was being considered. The prototype was nicknamed 'Gladys' due to its slightly heavy looking lower body line, which was cribbed directly from the P6. The car was used as a personal hack by Bache for a number of years.

At the time of writing, the car was in the care of the British Motor Museum in Gaydon, Warwickshire. Even with its Rover 2-litre 4-cylinder overhead camshaft engine rather than the Rover V8, with its fully up to date independent front suspension, sliding tube de Dion rear end and a luxuriously appointed interior, the Alvis GTS was an attractive looking, relatively sporting and sophisticated car which would have been a worthy successor to the TF21.

Rover P6BS

The second postscript was for a more overtly sporting mid-engined 'Alvis' model, the Rover P6BS two-door coupé. The car was developed during 1967 by the Rover New Vehicle Projects Team and incorporated a very neat and clever transmission system designed by Alvis. The car was built

The Rover P6 provided the platform for the GTS, which resulted in a slightly heavy looking rear quarter.

From the front, the Alvis GTS had a modern appearance, with large rectangular headlamps behind Perspex covers and neatly integrated side lights. The bonnet had bulges to provide clearance for a Rover V8 engine, but the prototype was powered by a Rover 2000 4-cylinder engine.

The prototype and only Alvis GTS was built by London-based coachbuilder Radford.

The Rover **P6BS** was a mid-engined coupé with a clever transmission system developed by Alvis engineers after the Rover takeover.

While essentially a prototype for use in technology development, the **P6BS** was built to a production standard. The Rover V8's twin SU carburettors were covered with a Perspex bubble to keep the rear deck height as low as possible.

From the front, the P6BS has a purposeful look, with no grille and the air intake under the bumper – trends that production cars would follow.

at Alvis's Holyhead Road factory. The P6BS was a prototype two-door coupé with a mid-mounted Rover V8 engine, independent front suspension, de Dion rear suspension and ample room for two passengers and their luggage.

The car was built to production standards, but the Leyland Group, which had bought Standard-Triumph in 1960 and Rover in 1967, had reviewed the Rover portfolio and decided not to give the go-ahead to produce the P6BS, due to the then current production commitments. However, the project was kept alive as a development and experimental car. With its angular boxy styling, the P6BS could be considered to be a link between the organic, curved styling of the 1950s and 1960s and the more straight-line 'wedge' approach of the 1970s, which gives the car a unique if slightly awkward appearance. However, the three-box styling was distinct and neat, and with a pronounced low waistline crease running between the front and rear wheels, oblong headlamps recessed into the front panel, a thin vertical air intake behind the door pillar to feed air into the engine bay and a long, relatively low rear deck, the P6BS was certainly different. The bodyshell was a true monocoque, with load-bearing outer panels, box-section sills and a large luggage boot placed behind the engine compartment. Up front, the radiator was fitted in the nose and was angled forward about 55 degrees from the vertical, with an electric fan mounted above it.

The front suspension was fitted into a welded-in sub-frame and comprised a bolted upper wishbone, while the lower wishbone was a transverse link, which used the front-mounted anti-roll bar as its radius arm. The bottom of the coaxial spring and damper assembly bolted on to the lower transverse link, the fabricated sheet steel upright pivoted on ball joints and the front hub carried a disc brake. The fuel tank was positioned low down between the front suspension behind the radiator just in front of the wheel axis. The spare wheel was mounted on top of the tank. The steering rack was mounted behind the axle line and was positioned high up on the scuttle, operating on the top of the suspension uprights. The cabin was neatly laid out with standard Rover P6 instruments and was fully trimmed to production standards.

A pair of vestigial rear seats was built into the rear of the cabin, which would have been suitable for children only. The

This shot shows the contrasting rear ends of the **GTS** and the **P6BS**.

The **P6BS** interior was fully fitted out and gives the car a sporty look and feel.

The rear end of the **P6BS** is fairly square and neat. The Perspex cover over the carburettors is an obvious indicator that this is a prototype.

The Managing Director of Red Triangle, Richard Joyce, poses beside a classic 1930s Alvis in the Red Triangle workshops.

3.5-litre Rover V8 was fitted behind the cabin and was offset 6.125in (155.6mm) to the right, so that the differential could be fitted centrally to allow the use of equal length drive-shafts. In order to keep the weight distribution as close to the centre of the car as possible, the engine was turned 180 degrees so that it faced backwards. The P6 gearbox was laid on its side and mounted in front of and below the engine, so that it actually sat underneath the rear seats. Drive from the engine to the gearbox was by a Hy-Vo chain, which ran from a sprocket mounted in front of the clutch to the gearbox layshaft. The output from the gearbox was by an extended main shaft that ran down the left-hand side of the engine to the differential.

The differential casing was cast integrally with the engine sump, but did not share the oil, and thanks to the engine's offset mounting was central to the car. The rear suspension was an adaptation of the P6's de Dion set-up, with the de Dion tube widened by 1.5in (38mm) to suit the car's wider track. The Rover V8 was fed by a pair of SU carburettors that were housed under a Perspex bulge in the top of the boot lid. While the P6BS never made it into production, it was a neat, sophisticated and not unattractive coupé that represented another lost opportunity for Leyland and then British Leyland.

RED TRIANGLE

When Alvis stopped making cars in 1967, it still wanted to provide spares and mechanical support to its loyal customers, so the Alvis Passenger Car division was set up and relocated to a site in Kenilworth. Red Triangle's ethos is to ensure that Alvis customers continue to receive specialist support for their cars. The new entity took all the existing Alvis car works drawings and technical data sheets, as well as the customer correspondence files and dispatch books, along with the factory's stocks of spares. So Red Triangle has the capability to remake virtually any Alvis part and currently holds stocks of many parts for Alvis cars.

The company offers a range of services to Alvis owners, from carrying out routine servicing, doing more involved mechanical work such as engine rebuilds (it has its own engine test bed), as well as bodywork and interior trim repair and fixing crash damage. It also offers restoration services and has the skills to rebuild and restore any Alvis bodywork, carry out chassis and mechanical repairs and paint to high standards. The company will also buy and sell Alvis cars of all ages.

Red Triangle has developed a number of enhancements that can be fitted to customers' cars, ranging from cylinder

Alvis owners and their clubs are enthusiastic, friendly and welcoming. Here is a 12/50 'Woody' and a 3.5-litre at a wet Newlands Corner meeting.

heads suitable for unleaded fuel, discrete power-assisted steering systems and overdrive systems that reduce engine revs by up to 22 per cent in top gear.

Red Triangle works closely with the new Alvis Car Company and will hand-build a modern Alvis from scratch. Working from the original Alvis drawings and specifications, the new cars are designed to meet the UK's Single Vehicle Approval regulations – see http://www.thealviscarcompany.co.uk

Red Triangle is based at Common Lane, Kenilworth, Warwickshire, CV8 2EL and its website is www.redtriangle.co.uk

ALVIS CLUBS AND RESOURCES

The Alvis Owner Club was founded in 1951 and caters for the owners of all Alvis vehicles, including the military vehicles. The club's objective is: 'the preservation of Alvis vehi-

cles, the running of social and competitive events for all Alvis vehicle enthusiasts and in so far as is practical, providing services to members'.

The club is run by a board of directors and has a worldwide presence, as it is divided into a number of UK and overseas sections, each of which is run by its own committee and organizes events that are open to all members. Each year, the club organizes an International Alvis Weekend, when members from the UK and overseas attend. The club publishes a bimonthly journal, *The Bulletin*, which covers club activities, Alvis history and what is happening in the Alvis world.

With a useful website (http://alvisoc.org) and an active membership, the club is an important resource for the Alvis owner and enthusiast. General enquiries can be addressed by email at enquiries@alvisoc.org, and the postal address Alvis Owner Club Limited, Eversheds House, 70 Great Bridgewater Street, Manchester M1 5ES.

A TD21 at a Brooklands New Year's Day meet.

The Alvis Register is the club for owners and people with an interest in the Alvis cars produced in the vintage era, that is, between 1919 and 1933. The Register's ethos is to: 'encourage and assist owners to enjoy their cars to the full, and for most members the enjoyment is in using, driving and maintaining the cars as Alvis intended'.

To this end, the Alvis Register has a spares scheme, gives technical advice, runs local events and workshop weekends, publishes a monthly *Circular* and quarterly *Bulletin* and has access to original Alvis handbooks and parts lists. Contact with the Alvis Register is via its website, http://www.alvis-register.co.uk

The Alvis Archive was set up in 2002, when the Alvis Owner Club established a legal trust to preserve the many Alvis-related photographs, documents, correspondence, drawings and other printed matter that the club had acquired over the years. Based at Bowcliff Hall, Bramham, LS23 6LP, the trust also runs a website, https://alvisarchive.com, on which it has placed a lot of information.

For Alvis front-wheel drive cars, Tony Cox (see Chapter 3) runs a website named after the shims used on the ohc engines of the FWD cars, http://hells-confetti.com. This gives a huge amount of information on the road and race cars and includes lots of technical details.

BIBLIOGRAPHY

Bardsley, Gillian, *Issigonis – The Official Biography* (London: Icon Books). Biography of Alec Issigonis, including a chapter on his time at Alvis.

Basnett, Fred, *Travels of a Capitalist Lackey* (London: George Allen and Unwin Ltd). Published in 1965, this book details the travels of the author in a 1926 Alvis 12/50. The epic 10,000-mile trip started and finished in London and covered Sweden, Norway, Finland, the USSR, Turkey, the Balkans, Austria, Germany, France and back to London. An amusing and eventful travelogue in a vintage Alvis.

Clarke, R.M., *Alvis – Gold Portfolio 1919–1967* (Cobham: Brooklands Books). Compilation of magazine road tests and model introductions from the British motoring press.

Culshaw, David, *Alvis Three Litre in Detail* (Beaworthy: Herridge and Sons). A comprehensive and well-illustrated view of the post-war Three-Litre Alvis.

Day, Kenneth, *Alvis – The Story of the Red Triangle, 2nd Edition* (Yeovil: Haynes Publishing Group). Comprehensive history of the Alvis company, its cars, armoured vehicles and aero engines.

Fox, John, *Alvis Cars 1946–1967: The Post-War Years* (Stroud: Amberley Publishing). Concise and well-illustrated guide to the post-war Alvis cars.

Hull, Peter, *The Front-Wheel-Drive Alvis*, Profile Publications Number 51. Pamphlet covering the 1920s front-wheel drive road and racing cars.

Hull, Peter and Johnson, Norman, *The Vintage Alvis* (privately published by the Alvis Register). Covers the history of the company and its cars up to 1930.

Munro, Bill, *Alvis Saracen Family* (Ramsbury: The Crowood Press). A comprehensive history and description of the six-wheel drive Alvis fighting vehicles.

Nicholson, T.R., *The Alvis Speed 20 & 25, 3½ & 4.3 Litre Models*, Profile Publications Number 11. Pamphlet covering the pre-war 6-cylinder models.

Price Williams, John, *Alvis – The Postwar Cars* (Croydon: Motor Racing Publications Ltd). History of the post-war Alvis cars.

Probert, Roy, *'Leonides' The Alvis Aero Engine* (Waterloo, IA: Levante Publishing). History of the Alvis aero engines.

Taylor, Clive, *Alvis Cars in Competition* (Stroud: Amberley publishing). This book looks at many of the current existing Alvis models that have a competition history and gives a brief rundown of their history.

Walker, Nick, *Alvis Speed Models in Detail* (Beaworthy: Herridge and Sons). A well-illustrated book on the Speed 20, Speed 25, 3½-litre and 4.3-litre models.

Ward, Rod, *Alvis Album, An Auto Review Book* (Zetec Publishing). Pocket guide to the Alvis and its history.

INDEX